Relate is here for people who want to make their family relationships better.

We help people make sense of what's happening in their relationships, decide what they want to do and make those changes.

In addition to our respected and popular range of books, we have many other ways to support people. Our counsellors are trained professionals. You can have a local appointment with a counsellor face-to-face, on the phone or consult them online through our website. We also run counselling for children in primary and secondary schools and in our Relate centres, as well as relationship courses and workshops.

We work with couples, families and individuals. Our network reaches across the whole of the UK, where we are the largest provider of relationship support and sex therapy.

Find more relationship advice and information about our services on our website at www.relate.org.uk or call us on 0300 100 1234.

Barbara Bloomfield is a couples and family counsellor and supervisor who has been with Relate since 1994. She has written several books and booklets on relationships and social history, including *The Dating Game* for London Weekend Television. Barbara teaches at Bath Spa University where she took a master's degree in creative writing. Barbara can be contacted at: www.inspireparents.com/finding-love

The Relate Guide to Finding Love

Barbara Bloomfield

relate

Vermilion
LONDON

3 5 7 9 10 8 6 4

Published in 2009 by Vermilion, an imprint of Ebury Publishing

Ebury Publishing is a Random House Group company

The Random House Group Limited Reg. No. 954009

Addresses for companies within the Random House Group can be
found at: www.randomhouse.co.uk

A CIP catalogue record for this book is available
from the British Library

Penguin Random House is committed to a sustainable future for
our business, our readers and our planet. This book is made from
Forest Stewardship Council® certified paper.

Printed and bound in Great Britain by Clays Ltd, St Ives plc

ISBN 9780091923976

Copies are available at special rates for bulk orders. Contact the sales
development team on 020 7840 8487 for more information.

To buy books by your favourite authors and register for offers, visit
www.randomhouse.co.uk

This book is a work of non-fiction. The names of people in the case
studies have been changed solely to protect the privacy of others.

Contents

Acknowledgements

Biggest thanks go to Margaret Hickman, co-author of Chapter 3. Margaret, an experienced life coach, has been the best possible writing colleague, always ready with ideas, inspiration and witty encouragement. Many thanks also to Ruth Yudkin for writing the section on gay dating, and to Mary Balfour, Cath Allen, Peter Bell, Kari Channell, Julia Kellaway and Michele Turney for their wise advice and many suggestions.

Very big thanks to all the individuals who generously gave their time to talk about love triumphs and terrors: Alice C, Martin B, Maria, Michael, Colston, Gill, Debbie, Syaed, Tina, Anna, Eva, Martin P and Fiona. The love stories told to me by Tina, Gemma, Reg and the other young stylists at Moda were an inspiration! Margaret would like to thank Jacqui Ramsey, Emma, Annie and Trevor for their generous help.

Finally, thanks to Relate Avon and to our families, Ben, Livvy, Zoë and Anna and John and Joey.

Introduction

➤ Are you ready to find love again?

➤ Do you need to move on from a break-up?

➤ Do you want help finding your Mr/Ms Right?

➤ Are you ready to look at previous relationships to see what went wrong?

If the answer to any of these questions is yes, you're in the right place. This book's mission is to help you feel confident about finding a new partner. Most of the reasons for lack of success will be something you can actively change. It might be that past experiences have lowered your confidence or that you are giving out off-putting signals. Perhaps loss and sadness have taken you over, making it difficult for you to think about finding another partner. Maybe you need help attracting the right type of person. On the other hand, you might get to the end of this book and discover that you really enjoy being single and don't need someone special to share your life. If that's the case, great!

When a leading national newspaper commissioned me to join six introduction agencies and go on 27 dates to research the effectiveness of their matchmaking, I'm sure they didn't realise it was going to be money wasted. I didn't find Mr Right or even Mr Not Too Bad, and no-one seemed to think I was Ms Right either.

Instead, I spent one long evening in a pub with a man who compiled telephone directories for a living and had brought along the Bs to Ds so that we could look at them together. Another surreal afternoon was spent with someone who wanted to show me pictures of *all* his mansions in California and the helicopters he kept there for his international travel. There was also one nice guy with a ponytail and a sense of humour who I never called back because I was too shy and terrified of rejection. Mind you, he never called me back either – I wonder if it was for the same reason? Looking back I can see that, like the dates I was meeting, I wasn't in the right place emotionally to find a new love. I'd recently had a bad split with someone and felt like one of the 'walking wounded', much too defensive and touchy to let myself fall for anyone.

A few years later, back on the love trail, romance felt less desperate and a lot more fun – or maybe it was me who was in a better place. Friends were answering adverts in the personal columns and having a great time meeting unemployed Belgians or Bolivian psychoanalysts. My gay and bisexual friends were enjoying a similar flowering and coming out into a gay dating scene that was as colourful as it was friendly and exploratory.

Then along came the Internet and, with the spread of personal computers, the romance scene changed again. Almost overnight, online dating websites started popping up catering to all kinds of niche markets. Within five minutes of going online, you could be chatting with someone who apparently shared your hobbies, tastes and preferences. I say 'apparently' because things are never quite what they seem on the Internet, as we shall find out.

So with this never-ending supply of PPM (Potential Partner Material) it must be easy to find love, romance and marriage, right? Wrong. Just look around at your circle of friends. How many of them are finding it hard to meet a genuine partner who doesn't drop them after one or two dates? How many of them are saying: 'There's no-one out there for me'? How many are regularly having dating disasters, funny and not so funny: the one whose false teeth fell out onto the table; the exciting e-mailer with the false name who turned out to be her ex-husband; the man who seemed so keen on the phone and never showed up; the shy, sincere woman who turned out to have a husband and five children?

These true stories make entertaining tales after the event, but most of us care so deeply about finding love and companionship in a harsh world that these dating disasters seem to cover up some of the pain we feel when a relationship doesn't work out.

GETTING THE MOST FROM THIS BOOK

To get the most from our plan, we recommend you go out and purchase a journal to make notes in. Any department store will have a selection in luscious colours and patterns to choose from. Select one that looks and feels really good for you, and perhaps choose a pen too.

In your journal you will be writing down details of potential partners who have caught your eye. In addition, you will be learning a lot about yourself along the way by completing some exercises and quizzes. These can be fun and illuminating about your strengths and the inner conflicts or worries that are holding you back. Although you may be tempted to skip over the exercises, taking the time to do them will help you get the most from the book.

We also want you to find yourself a close friend who you can share your experiences with and confide in. This friend

– male or female – must be someone you trust and wants only the best for you. In an ideal world, he or she might be someone who is also looking for love so you can support each other. You will want your friend to be a good listener so that you can share your experiences, a motivator who can jolly you up when times get difficult and an empathiser who can reflect with understanding on your feelings.

IS THIS BOOK FOR YOU?

At Relate we welcome and work with all clients, whatever their sexual preferences – gay, straight or bisexual. The gay romantic scene is so huge and international that much has already been written about it, but we have been keen to include some information and personal experiences from gay and bisexual daters. For ease, we've tended to concentrate on heterosexual and female daters but I hope any man or gay person reading this will find plenty of interest and food for thought in these pages and that it will spur you to take inspired action whatever your love interest may be.

The book is aimed at women and men who are interested in forming longer-term and committed relationships or marriage. If you are looking for a casual or a sexual relationship, there is no shortage of adult sites on the Internet where you can find people looking 'just for fun' and you probably don't need our help. However, this book *is* for you if:

➤ you're looking for something longer-lasting, together with a better understanding of your family background and the values and experiences that have made you who you are

➤ you want to learn something about the psychology of relationships

➤ you would like to overcome your personal barriers to finding love, marriage and friendship by embarking on a feel-good programme that will give you the best chance of success

Once you start doing something proactive, even if it's a very small change in your normal routine, you open up new possibilities. So let's get going.

Chapter 1

The Search for Love

LOVE IS . . .?

. . . such a big subject. It's complicated and simple at the same time. We think we recognise it when it strikes us like a thunderbolt out of nowhere but then, like a storm, it can pass overhead quickly, leaving us wondering what happened. But if you go looking for it, romantic love can be the hardest thing to find: maddening, slippery and just out of reach.

Love is a basic need for human survival, as important as food and shelter. Without the love and protection of its parents, a child won't thrive. Psychologists say this need to thrive, grow and better ourselves is a feature of our adult relationships and particularly of the search for romantic love. In the love of an adult partner we see a chance to become better people, to expand the range of our experiences and learn new things. And perhaps it's the highly risky nature of romantic love – our knowledge that we are as likely to fail as to succeed in our quest to grow as human beings – that makes it so special and prized, the inspiration for the finest songs, stories, poetry and books throughout human history.

In English, we use one word to describe a whole range of feelings, from the passionate to the tender, but the ancient Greeks used at least three different words to mean love. 'Eros' meant passionate love, with sensual desire and long-ing. It is where the word 'erotic' comes from, although eros was more concerned with the beauty inside a person than their physical attractiveness. The inner beauty of eros was said to be the inspiration for ancient philosophers and artists to seek the truth. 'Philia' was their name for a general love of family and friends, and loyalty to your community. Philia could also be felt between lovers. The third type, 'agape', means 'love' in modern Greek. In the ancient world it was used to suggest tender feelings for one's children and towards a spouse. It suggests holding people in high regard and being content with them.

Eros is the kind of love that gets all the attention today because sex gets a lot of headlines! But love in the more general sense is the hardest thing to describe in English because it encompasses several different kinds of love: the passion of lovers; the tenderness of a parent for a child; the wider love for your fellow humans. What's missing, perhaps, is the modern idea of loving and valuing ourselves, although we note that people who like and accept themselves tend to have love to spare and create a cycle of loving behaviour around them. The opposite is also true: people who don't feel good about themselves, for whatever reason, will sometimes struggle to generate a warm and loving relationship.

The following quotes from women and men who were interviewed for this book show a great range of thoughts about this deceptively simple question: what is love?

'Love feels like a great whoosh of excitement, longing, fear and desire.'

'Love is being respected by a partner to be left alone to be yourself.'

'Love is wanting to spend time with someone, over and above other people.'

'To me, love is a four-letter word closely linked to another four-letter word, fear.'

'Love is a temporary insanity but easily cured by marriage.'

'The only love I can define is being willing to die for my daughter. That's clearly love.'

'Love is being connected by a silk thread; being tugged against your will to merge with another human being and forget yourself.'

'Love is when you feel really satisfied and secure with another.'

'Love is when he says he loves me.'

'Love is a positive force for good. It's not sentimental but has huge creative energy.'

'Love is really about loving yourself and then letting it flood out to the world.'

Love is . . . more complex than a Valentine's Day slogan. How would you define it?

WHAT DO YOU WANT FROM A RELATIONSHIP?

We have seen that the word 'love' can mean many things to different people – security, passion, nurturing, excitement, stability, respect. Indeed, it can mean all of the above at different moments in a relationship. In the same way, there are many reasons why an individual might want to change their circumstances and take a chance on finding love.

At Relate, each client is special and unique. However, they often come for help with love problems at certain stressful or crisis points in their lives when they have become aware of being lonely, isolated or that they are missing something. For example:

➤ A young adult who wants to find a partner but feels afraid of closeness or sex or thinks they are 'no good at relationships'.

➤ A woman or man in their late 20s/early 30s who suddenly finds themselves alone after parting from someone they met while at school or college.

➤ Someone in their 20s or 30s who has moved away from home and is alone in a new city, or perhaps worrying that their biological clock is running out if they want to have children.

➤ A single parent whose children have hit milestones, such as going to school for the first time or leaving home. They may be experiencing 'empty nest' feelings and be a little fearful.

➤ An individual grieving for the end of a marriage who is trying to claw back their self-esteem and a sense of hope that they can be happy again.

➤ A client who needs to talk about and grieve the death of a partner before they can think of loving again.

All these moments of crisis are big life events involving loss, sadness and fear. However, they are also milestones that hold the seeds of hope for learning, growing and finding future happiness and love. Let's look in more detail at some of the stories behind these life-stage changes.

'I'm Single Again and Terrified.' Emma, 36

The last time Emma was single, she was 19, and she finds lots of things have changed since then.

Coming out of a 16-year relationship is scary. From the safe and comfortable position of being in a long-term relationship, I watched my bright and beautiful 30-something friends grapple with the reality of trying to find and meet new men in the modern world.

Now I am one of them and full of fear and trepidation about what the world of dating might be like. Not only am I worried that in the last 16 years my appearance has changed as I have grown older, acquired scars, altered my shape and dress size and generally become less visually appealing than I once was, but that now the rules of how to date have fundamentally changed too!

I'm worried that even if a man did find me in any way attractive, he might not have the confidence to let me know. In the past, I found men to be confident about approaching women. As a group of young single girls, we would often go to bars, clubs or parties and expect that during the evening one or all of us would be chatted up. The unspoken rule was that the men would make the first move, ask you to dance, buy you a drink, come over to talk to you and so on. You may have given them an encouraging smile but generally the ball was in their court.

My single friends say older men are more self-conscious about talking to women or more cautious about what the response might be. Also, as we all grow older together, we become settled and secure in our friendship groups and less keen to step outside them to get to know someone new. Whatever the reasons, it is no longer enough to go down to your local bar and expect to meet and date someone new!

My friends think Internet dating is the way forward. Although the idea fills me with dread and horror, I cannot deny they have had lots of fun and met a wide selection of interesting, witty and available new men. Obviously, not all the men they have met have been great, but they have gained lots of dating experience and are now able to tell hilarious stories at parties. When I have taken enough time to recover from my separation and have rebuilt my confidence and self-esteem, then no doubt I will also be taking that first shaky step into the world of Internet dating.

Once I decided to end my relationship, it was a huge relief and I felt physically lighter. However, the reality of being on my own and what that would mean in the long run was almost paralysing. Knowing that I would now have to take full responsibility for all my decisions in life was a bit overwhelming but also challenging in an exciting way.

I worry about how a new relationship will fit into the things I value so much in my life, such as my career and my circle of friends. I also worry about what men will think of me now. I never really flirted or dated men before I was 19. Now I am in a strange position of being single, 36 years old and being taught the subtleties of flirting by my friends. I hope it is not too late.

As Emma found, it can be terrifying coming out of a long-term relationship. With a partner you get used to feeling secure about yourself; what you believe, how you look, speak and feel. When you are on your own you suddenly worry that maybe you are not who you thought you were. Maybe other people will not see all those qualities you thought you had or, on a bad day, you might doubt you ever had any qualities at all.

Being in a relationship is like having a security blanket wrapped around you: whatever happens during the day, there will be someone who cares and will listen to you when you get home. When you're single, it can feel that it's just you who will be there at the end of the day, and that can be exciting, scary or lonely.

Emma also wonders how she will integrate a new partner into her busy and successful life. Like many of us, having found an interesting career and a great group of friends, she doesn't want to compromise her life by getting into a relationship which limits her freedom to express herself. Maybe she should trust her instincts and believe that a good partnership will allow her freedom and the security that comes with having someone special in your life. Part of the excitement of developing a committed relationship is negotiating the tricky stuff and enjoying the give and take, the compromise and the firmness that you need to forge a strong relationship.

Like Emma, many people feel very anxious about getting into serious relationships. What they have in common is a terrible fear:

➤ fear of exposing yourself

➤ fear of remembering what you have lost

➤ fear of being rejected and being exposed to more pain

➤ fear of never finding a good-enough partner

➤ fear of family disapproval

➤ fear of children's disapproval

➤ fear of not being attractive enough

➤ fear of taking a chance on loving again

The fear is real but who wants to spend the rest of their life living in fear? This book will give you some tools and strategies for overcoming your fears and finding the courage to love again.

HOW DO YOU WANT TO LIVE?

Are you ready for a relationship? You may have woken up one morning and felt that the time was right or maybe you're not quite sure. To help you make that decision, consider your current circumstances, both emotional and practical. For instance, are you pining for a long-term, committed relationship or horrified at the thought of leaving your home and moving in with someone else? If you have children, how will that affect the partner you hope to attract? Will they be prepared to get involved in family life or would it be better all round to have a part-time relationship for companionship and fun?

Your present circumstances and past experiences will dictate the sort of marriage or relationship you want to have and what is possible. You may be tied to a certain location by your job, your family or by children's schooling. Or you might be completely the opposite: free, fed up with suburbia and dying to sail off into a Caribbean sunset.

The trouble is, we're not used to being 'calculating' about who we meet or thinking strategically about a future partner, and you might rebel against planning things so carefully. But if you were buying a new sofa, you'd have a pretty good idea what shape, colour, size and pattern you were looking for. Without being too picky, why not clarify in your mind what's possible in a new relationship and the sort of partner that would be best for you? If you know what you want you are more likely to find it.

You may be planning to go on blind dates but, whatever you do, don't date blindly or you could waste a lot of time, energy and money. Some of the experienced daters out there take this to crazy extremes. You will recognise them because they don't waste time on polite chat but are likely to welcome you to a first date in the same manner as the dater whose opening words were: 'Hello Lydia, I'm looking for a wife.'

Then there was another forthright dater who always put her cards on the table on the first date:

'I'm looking for an LAT.'

'What's that?' asked her mystified guest.

'A Living Apart Together arrangement, for fun, sex and companionship but we're never going to live in the same house,' she answered.

These kinds of insensitive daters are extremely off-putting to the majority of us, but they certainly know their own minds!

Take a few minutes now to think about the kind of relationship you're looking for. Here are some possibilities to consider:

➤ A light-hearted sexual relationship

➤ A romantic relationship without sex

➤ A best friend who's a lover

➤ Someone I can go on holiday with but keep my independence

➤ Marriage

➤ Living together

➤ A part-time or full-time relationship with separate homes

➤ A committed relationship in which we will have children

➤ A committed relationship in which to raise my existing children

➤ A full relationship without children or other baggage

➤ I'm not sure yet! Ask me in a while

➤ Having thought about it, I'd prefer to stay single

➤ Something else

If you're not sure of the answer right now, come back to this question later. Feel free to change your mind as you work through the book.

WHY DID YOUR LAST RELATIONSHIP END?

Spend a few minutes thinking or writing about your last relationship and why it ended. Was there a moment or an event that caused a crisis and brought things to a head? Or did it fizzle out slowly? Did you notice any similarities between your relationship and that of your parents or other members of your family? The following list may help to get you thinking about what went wrong:

➤ He/she treated me like a child and wouldn't let me grow up.

➤ We argued like mad and he/she got fed up with it.

➤ He/she found the relationship too boring and sex went off.

➤ We never seemed to be able to dovetail our moods or decide how we wanted to spend our time.

➤ He/she was too lazy: I had to push or nag all the time.

➤ He/she left me.

➤ Sex was fantastic but the relationship soon fizzled out: it was too much, too soon.

➤ She/he was terrified of closeness, sex and intimacy.

➤ She/he was physically or emotionally abusive or violent.

➤ My partner died.

➤ I've never had a romantic relationship before.

➤ One of us wanted children; the other didn't.

➤ We had nothing in common.

➤ He/she had an affair.

➤ At first his/her jealousy was flattering. Later, I got annoyed by it.

➤ We disliked each other's friends/families/children.

➤ Money caused a problem between us.

➤ Another reason . . .

That last list might have been more about your ex-partner's faults. Now do something a little more challenging: have an honest think about **why YOU find relationships difficult**. Again, here's a list to get started:

➤ I fear rejection or getting hurt again.

➤ I'm too shy, awkward and tongue-tied.

➤ I fear losing control and making a fool of myself.

➤ I fear that I'm not attractive enough.

➤ I get too needy and clingy when I'm in a relationship.

➤ I'm afraid of intimacy and/or sex.

➤ I'm too choosy and critical of a partner.

➤ I seem to pick very difficult partners who aren't good for me.

➤ I seem to sabotage relationships through handling them badly.

➤ I never meet anyone I fancy.

➤ I'm used to being single and not sure how a new partner would fit into my life.

➤ I don't think there are any available men/women for me.

➤ I'm not sure I want to have a romantic partnership.

➤ Another reason . . .

THINKING ABOUT SEPARATION OR DIVORCE

Losing a partner is one of life's most painful and upsetting events. Whether or not you wanted to split, the transition from coupledom to being single again takes months or, for some people, years. On top of that is the loss of someone who was once your best friend, lover and companion, and perhaps the loss of your home as well as the end of all your hopes for that future relationship.

If your ex has engineered the split, you have to cope with feelings of rejection and the loss of self-esteem that comes with being abandoned. At Relate, we believe it can take around two years for each party to come to terms with the end of an important relationship; often, the rejected party won't really understand why the split is happening or may be trying to play 'catch up' with a decision that their partner has known about for some time. The feelings of rejection and betrayal can be overwhelming, and you need plenty of time to recover your sense of self and self-esteem. Treating yourself gently, looking after yourself and asking friends for support will all help at this difficult time.

Although losing a partner through separation or divorce isn't the same as when a partner dies, the stages of grief are almost identical for any serious loss. Grieving is a process of emotional adjustment during which powerful emotions conflict with each other. They don't happen one after the other but in a kind of cyclone of feelings that swirl around you, buffeting you backwards and forwards in grief. They become mixed up and unpredictable. One day will be better than another. You start to feel a little better, then suddenly find yourself plunged back into an earlier stage.

Those suffering from loss and grief after a break-up may recognise some of the following stages and phrases:

Shock. People say: 'I can't believe it' It may take you a long time to grasp what has happened. Some people will carry on as if nothing has happened. It is hard to believe that someone important is not coming back.

Numbness. People say: 'I feel nothing' The shock can make you numb, as if you're losing touch with reality.

Disbelief. People say: 'This can't be happening!' The loss seems cruel and unbelievable. If your partner has left suddenly, you will be looking for answers but perhaps not getting any.

Pain. People say: 'I can't bear the pain' The physical and mental distress involved in parting from a loved one can be overwhelming and extremely frightening.

Anger. People say: 'It's not fair. Why did it have to happen to me?' Those experiencing loss and grief will have bouts of extreme anger towards their partner.

Repetition of events. People say: 'I go over it again and again in my head' You can't help thinking about what happened and if you could have changed things.

Guilt. People say: 'If only . . .' You may feel guilty about things you could have done or said differently and want to turn back the clock.

Depression. People say: 'Life has no meaning, I can't go on' When the truth starts to sink in, the grief-stricken often feel depressed and that they don't want to carry on living.

Impatience. People say: 'How long is this pain going to last?' The head may be saying you've had enough of the crying and the pain, but your body won't obey. It can take over a year for the most severe symptoms to lessen, sometimes much longer.

Swimming across. People say: 'I want to forget him/her by dating again' An understandable attempt to 'swim across' from pain to happiness but is it too soon to make the crossing? Relationships that happen 'on the rebound' often fail and can leave you feeling very low.

Unpredictability. People say: 'One minute I'm angry and the next minute I can't stop crying' The mood swings can be very frightening and unpredictable.

Hope. People say: 'I think I'm feeling more myself again' A sense of looking to the future with hope starts to re-emerge in your daily life.

After a great loss, no-one can tell you when you are ready and able to start seeing a new future again. Try to do something small every day to remind yourself that you can and will be happy again, such as phoning a friend for a chat or taking a country walk. Our suggestions in Chapter 3 are designed to help you set small targets which will give you a sense of achievement when things seem bleak.

Chapter 2

How Well Do You Know Yourself?

Your upbringing can become a 'blueprint' for how you handle adult relationships and interact with your partner. Let's look at the part played by your family and the kinds of relationships you grew up with. These are probably the biggest indicator of your likely relationship with love.

Nobody is completely defined by their family but the way your parents (or whoever brought you up) handled the giving and receiving of love and affection inside the family is the biggest indicator of how you will relate to love. You cannot escape the unwritten messages about relationships that you absorbed during all those years of your growing up.

I can already hear the cries of those saying: 'Rubbish! I want something entirely different to my parents' relationship, which I remember as being so-so/angry/lacking in affection. I've put the experiences of my childhood behind me and I don't need to go back there to rake it up again.'

It's true that lots of us try and correct the messages we received from our upbringing and create more loving and stable relationships for ourselves. But, as Relate counsellors who work with many couples with relationship difficulties, we cannot help but frequently see patterns of attachment – both helpful and not so helpful – flowing from grandparents to parents and parents to children, however hard individuals might try not to repeat them.

At moments of stress and crisis these patterns can be especially noticeable as they become the 'default' setting that we fall into when we are under a great deal of pressure. For example, Megan noticed that when people raised their voices, she tended to withdraw and leave the room before any discussion or debate could get going. To hide under the table had been her childhood 'strategy' for dealing with her high-decibel parents, whose frequent and unpredictable arguments had scared her. But, as an adult, the withdrawal strategy was not helping her to grow as an individual because men saw her as a timid woman who shrank from interesting and lively discussions.

When you start to understand your love history and why you handle love and affection in a particular way, you're already halfway to making small changes for the better. In this chapter we've included some of the relationship theories we use inside Relate when we work with clients. If you find that you recognise some unhelpful patterns of thinking as a result of reading this chapter, you might want to consider talking to a counsellor who could help you to understand what's going on and to more forward. In a sense, this chapter looks backwards at the forces that have made you, while the next chapter looks ahead to the person you want to become and your potential to create the relationships you desire.

WHO DO YOU THINK YOU ARE?

Take hold of your journal and grab a pen. Think about your parents' relationship (or the relationships of the person who brought you up) and write short sentences to answer the following questions. There are no right or wrong answers. Try to write down your immediate reactions rather than what you believe you should think. When you've finished, think about the ways in which you have repeated, or tried to avoid repeating, certain elements of your upbringing. You might want to keep this private or discuss your thoughts with a friend.

LIFE STAGES

How did your parents/carers cope with big changes in their lives? For example:

➤ a new baby
➤ moving home
➤ kids going to school
➤ kids becoming teenagers
➤ your leaving home
➤ unemployment
➤ mid-life crisis
➤ an affair
➤ step-parents and step-siblings
➤ retirement
➤ unexpected illness
➤ bereavement

LOVE AND AFFECTION

How did you know your parents loved each other?
Did they kiss and show affection in front of you?
If not, why do you think they didn't?

SINGLE PARENT

If you were raised by a single parent or a carer, how did they feel about romantic relationships?
What messages did you pick up about love?

SEX

What messages did you get from your parents or step-parents about their sexual relationship?
How did this affect you as you grew up?

ANGER

Who was allowed to be angry in your family?
Who wasn't allowed to be angry?
Did they shout, sulk or hit out?
If no-one was angry, how did each person behave when they felt annoyed?

ANXIETY

How did your family handle stress?
Who was the most/least stressed person in the family?
Who looked after whom?
Who was good at calming themselves down?
What role did you play at stressful times?

CHANGE/CRISIS

Did things feel settled in your home?
Or was there separation, divorce or bereavement, or other major changes which unsettled you?
How did these affect you?

WORK AROUND THE HOME

What messages did you get about who did what?
What was 'man's work' and 'woman's work'?
Who did the cooking?

WORK OUTSIDE THE HOME

Whose job was regarded as more important?
Whose was less important?
What ideas did you get about earning a living?
Who handled the money/finances?

MOTTO

What would have been the motto above the door of your parents'/guardians' house that summed up their attitude to life?

WHAT IS YOUR ATTACHMENT STYLE?

Your answers to the last exercise will say quite a bit about the way you give and take affection and love with other people – family, friends and lovers. This is known as your 'attachment style'.

Attachment is a special emotional relationship involving the exchange of care, comfort and pleasure; it has been described as a lasting psychological connectedness between human beings. The view that early childhood experiences have an important influence on how we behave and develop as adults has been widely accepted since Sigmund Freud first suggested it at the beginning of the 20th century.

Psychoanalysts, like Freud, weren't saying that insecure children will necessarily become insecure adults or that secure children will always grow up to have loving relationships. The life experiences of individuals between childhood and adulthood, and their personality type, mean that there is potential for change in both directions.

Experts found that adults with different attachment styles

had different beliefs about relationships. In this context, a belief isn't necessarily about what you *know* you think (that is, what you'd like to believe) but about your below-the-surface, deeper values and how you act them out in everyday life. There's often quite a big gap between what we'd like to believe and what actually happens in our lives. For example, it's quite possible for a modern couple to *believe* that the household chores are shared equally between them whereas, in fact, one person is doing 90 per cent of the work and the other is doing 10 per cent.

The way you relate to others in terms of affection has been described as falling into three main styles: **secure, ambivalent** and **avoidant.**

Secure adults tend to have trusting, long-term relationships and to believe that romantic love lasts and endures. They have high self-esteem and enjoy talking about their feelings with other people. Securely attached children prefer the company of their own parents to strangers but don't become unduly upset by their absence. Parents of secure children play more with them and are more responsive to their needs.

Ambivalent adults report falling in love regularly and often but feel reluctant about getting close to others and worry that their partner doesn't feel as strongly in love as they do. As children they can be suspicious of strangers and hard to comfort but become dependent and clingy as they get older. Their self-esteem is easily dented and they tend to get distraught at the break-up of a relationship.

Avoidant attachers describe love as rare and temporary. They find casual sex easier to handle and don't disapprove of casual, short-term relationships. They find it hard to support their partner through difficult times and don't share their feelings easily. They may use excuses like tiredness and overwork to avoid sex and closeness. As children, they don't make emotional demands on their parents and can have a 'take it or leave it' attitude to affection.

Attachment styles can, to some extent, be 'passed' from one generation to the next. This is because attachment goes not just from the child to its parents but from the parent to the child, and the whole family develops a system of relating to each other. One study said that the likelihood of a parent passing on their own attachment style to their offspring is as high as 80 per cent.

Think about the way you gave and received love, both in your childhood and in adult relationships. What do you notice about your attachment style? Most people will find they are secure attachers, although all of us will show elements of the other styles at stressful times in our lives.

THREE TYPES OF RELATIONSHIP FIT

When we are on the lookout for a serious, long-term partner, psychologists believe we are trying to make three parts of a jigsaw come together in a social fit, a conscious fit and an unconscious fit.

THE SOCIAL FIT

The strict Victorian social divisions of upper, middle and lower class may be a thing of the past but we still look for partners of compatible social status. This means someone who probably has a similar educational, religious and class background to ourselves. We may have picked up subtle messages from our families about the kind of person they would like us to marry and, while some people rebel against this, most people tend to replicate the experiences they had when they were growing up.

THE CONSCIOUS FIT

If a friend were to ask why you fancy someone, your reply would be about the conscious fit. Status, looks, personality, wealth, humour, values, kindness and intelligence are the key features that draw us to fall in love with one person rather than another.

THE UNCONSCIOUS FIT

Have you ever found yourself at a party getting strong feelings about someone you've just met that are not based on physical attraction? Does this person you've just met feel like a 'kindred spirit'? Or do you know a couple who seem so completely unsuited to each other that none of their friends can puzzle out why they are together? If so, this could be the unconscious fit at work.

All of us carry with us a psychological patterning from our childhood, holding details about our life experiences and the marks they've left. It contains information we often haven't acknowledged about our fears and anxieties and how we cope with difficult feelings and situations. Each of us has an unconscious capacity to scan another person's blueprint. The people we're most attracted to are those who have a blueprint that is complementary to our own. We're looking for similarities of experience but, more significantly, we're also looking for differences.

The purpose of this unconscious fit is to find someone who can complement our experiences. That might be someone who's the same as us, but most commonly we're looking for someone who has developed coping mechanisms that are different from our own. Without being aware of this, we instinctively feel we have something to learn from these people we find especially attractive. The ideal fit will be someone who has struggled with similar life issues, but has developed another way of managing them. It seems that our other half is often our best chance of becoming psychologically whole.

Without realising it, couples tend to re-create situations that are unresolved from their childhoods. For example, if you weren't allowed to be angry in your family, you may unconsciously choose a partner whose family is more comfortable with being angry. In this way, your partner can 'do anger' on your behalf and you don't have to do it at all. This division or 'projection' of uncomfortable feelings tends to work until the point where individuals want to grow and develop for their own sake. Then the fit becomes more awkward and one will accuse the other person: 'You've changed!'

Types of Unconscious Fit

So although unconscious fits can make you feel 'whole' in the early stages of relationships, they start to fall apart when one part of the couple wants to grow and change. Unconscious fits that have outgrown their usefulness are probably the biggest reason for couples coming to Relate. What was once charming and attractive about someone ('He's so organised!' 'She's so caring!') can, over the years, turn into the very quality that drives you mad ('He's so controlling!' 'She's so flaky!'). See if you recognise any of the following four most common kinds popping up in your own relationships:

Net and Sword – the Shared Defence against Intimacy

Both partners are scared of being close and they find their perfect match in a partner who appears to be the opposite. The unspoken agreement is that one of them will keep pursuing and nagging the other for more intimacy while the other runs away or pretends they don't care. (Stereotypically, women tend to do the former and men the latter.) In counselling, this sort of couple can often switch the other way around, so when the reluctant partner comes towards his mate, the one who said she wanted more intimacy tends to take a step backwards. We sometimes call this a 'dance of intimacy'.

Babes in the Wood – the Shared Defence against Adventure

Just like the fairy tale where the children snuggled together in the nasty forest, covering themselves with leaves for protection, the babes in the wood couple keeps all the nice, cuddly things inside the relationship and puts all the bad in the evil world outside. They will like and dislike the same things, rarely venture out without each other and appear to friends to be joined at the hip. But this protective device that shelters them from reality comes at a price – often the sexual side of such relationships is poor because there is not enough tension and excitement to keep things interesting.

Cat and Dog – the Shared Defence against Loss of Identity

This couple does nothing but argue and is the absolute opposite of babes in the wood. Indeed, all their friends wonder why they are together. They try to get people to take their side and won't let up. And yet the cat and dog couple is, in reality, tightly bound together; they need the arguments in order to prove to themselves that they are individuals. By stating their differences they feel a sense of security about who they are as people. Typically, they enjoy their sexual relationship because they find the cycle of moving between closeness and distance to be exciting. However, it can all go wrong if one person decides they are bored with unproductive arguing and wants to change the pattern of interacting.

Parent/Child – the Shared Defence against Responsibility

Both parties collude so that one acts out the role of the child and the other becomes the parent figure. By doing this, the childlike partner never has to take control of their life, while the parental one never has to be dependent on another human being because their partner is acting out this role on their behalf. When it gets out of hand, parent/child can easily become a master/servant relationship that becomes abusive or violent.

Does this chapter raise ideas in your mind about the sort of relationships you tended to get into in the past or the kind of marriage you had? What new ideas are you having about the kind of person you are?

If you would like to think more deeply about these issues, try this more advanced exercise. Pick a time in your childhood, when you were 8, 10, 12 or whatever. Now imagine and write down what advice your adult self – the age you are now – would give to that child about life, love and marriage. What do you notice about that advice and all you have learned about life since you were a child? What do you think your child-self would say in reply, if you could give them a voice?

If it appeals, next try speaking with your future voice, as an 80-year-old you or a 100-year-old you. What wise words will you have about love as an old man or woman?

If you could hear his words, what advice would your great-grandson – who is yet to be born – give you about love?

If you managed to do that challenging exercise, congratulations on your imagination and think about taking a course in creative or therapeutic writing!

Any new ideas you are developing about what has made you the person you are today will be useful to take into the next chapter, which is about upping your confidence to begin the search for love.

Chapter 3

Loving Yourself, Loving Another

Wouldn't it be nice to think there is someone out there looking for someone like you? There is, but are you ready to take the inspired action to attract them into your life? For us to find love it helps if we first feel good about ourselves. In order to attract a loving partner who is happy and confident, we need to generate this feeling inside ourselves. In other words, love yourself and you will attract satisfying relationships.

This chapter gives you a **Positivity Plan** to boost your self-esteem. It has been put together with the help of life coach Margaret Hickman, an expert in dissolving the barriers we construct against hurt and disappointment.

WHAT IS SELF-ESTEEM?

High self-esteem is the ability to experience oneself as being able to cope with life's day-to-day challenges and to feel worthy of living a life of happiness and joy, appreciating ourselves and our value as a person. Many people have low self-esteem and lack self-confidence. This often means that they can lose hope of ever achieving what they want because they are not motivated to take the first inspired step to a more positive life. Feelings of helplessness, powerlessness and depression can follow.

If you are lacking in self-confidence it is so easy to get caught up in a negative spiral, typically by running an inner dialogue about not being good enough in some way or another. For women this may be connected to your appearance, such as: 'No-one's going to love me with my big feet/small breasts/big tummy.' Or it could be about a recent or distant past event which left you feeling ashamed, even though everyone else has forgotten about it. 'Why did I say . . . ?' 'Everyone thinks I'm an idiot because . . .' or 'If only I hadn't said . . . !' How often do you find yourself 'awfulising' – imagining that things are much worse than they actually are? If you think of these negative thoughts as a wheel going around and around in your head, then your task now is to jam a stick into that wheel and stop it spinning.

Having low self-esteem often goes hand in hand with searching for perfection in a potential partner. This may sound strange but, in fact, this combination provides a perfect barrier *against* getting involved in a new relationship because 'it'll end in disaster'. Perfectionism becomes a protective device put up to stop yourself taking a risk or getting hurt. Without being conscious of doing it, your mind says: 'Don't bother with this one – it's not going to be perfect.' You can easily see how this stops any worthwhile relationship from developing.

Negativity, perfectionism and anxiety are such everyday problems that you need to ask yourself at this moment: are you even ready for love? If the honest answer is 'not yet', spend a few weeks working out with our Positivity Plan before you start putting yourself out there.

THE POSITIVITY PLAN

The suggestions in our programme are small and easy bite-sized steps that you can take one at a time. Don't try to change too much at once. In fact, don't try too hard to change anything at all; just have a go at one of the steps; have a play and enjoy taking a small action in the spirit of 'this might be interesting'. There's no time limit to the steps and you can always go back and do an earlier step again, if you feel like it.

Friends sometimes get into the habit of enjoying long 'moaning' sessions and support each other by agreeing that 'life is terrible'. Although this provides a chance to off-load feelings, it doesn't shift a stuck pattern of negativity and self-doubt. So, if you are picking a friend to chat to about your search for love, don't choose a 'good moaner' or someone who is going to go along with everything you say. Choose the most positive person you know. Try and tell them what you need from them right from the start: to be a helper and motivator and someone to keep your spirits up. You are looking for someone who can 'pump the positive' – in other words, who can challenge any unflattering remarks you make about yourself and offer fresh ways of looking at life. They will be pleased that you see them in this way.

If there is no-one in your life that you can turn to or trust to fill this role, think about using a supportive networking site to find an online pal (you can remain anonymous while doing this if you want). This suggestion comes with a health warning to take care of your personal safety as people you meet on the Internet are not always all that they seem. The Appendix at the end of the book may be useful here (see page 173).

As you work through the steps in the programme, keeping a record of your thoughts and feelings will give you a sense of accomplishment. Writing down your thoughts can be difficult at first but, like all good things, it gets easier with practice, especially as no-one is 'judging' your efforts, and you don't have to share what you write with anyone if you don't want to.

STEP 1: SAY NO TO MIND CHATTER

We all have a huge amount of chatter going on in our heads all the time. This inner dialogue is often linked to negative emotions and laden with fear. It is our conscious mind talking to us and trying as hard as it can to preserve what it knows and with that its power. Our conscious mind fears silence and always looks to fill a vacuum as it chatters on about our faults. For the most part we are not aware that we can do something about it.

Has this sort of chatter been going on in your head for years?

'You're not good-looking.'
'You're really unsexy.'
'Call yourself fit!'
'You have no willpower.'
'Don't think anyone will fancy you.'
'You're a hopeless parent.'

It goes on and on. You need to get control of this dialogue before the chatter gets hold of you.

In your journal, write down all the mind chatter you experience, the good, the bad and the ugly. Don't censor yourself or keep crossing things out. Just write down whatever comes into your head, the negatives and the posi-tives. It doesn't have to make perfect sense. Let the words flow straight onto the paper. Carry on for as long as you want, and write as much as you can. Then shut your diary and put it away into a drawer overnight. This is important because if you read what you've written too soon, there's a chance you might get self-conscious and inhibited. When you read what you've written the next day, allow yourself to feel surprised and pleased by the achievement.

There are a number of ways to get some leverage over your thoughts. The easiest is to say out loud 'STOP STOP STOP' when the chatter starts, and then something positive like:

'I want to think differently.'
'I *do* like myself.'
'I can take control of my life.'
'I'm not listening to you any more.'

If it starts up again keep saying 'NO NO NO' and then feed back another positive comment. You might want to do this when you're alone or risk getting some odd looks! Eventually this practice will reduce the mind chatter and enable you to get some control over your thoughts so you start to think more positively. Become conscious of what your mind chatter is telling you and write it down in your journal. Then turn around this nasty, niggling voice into a positive statement.

Reinforce this by getting into the habit of speaking well of others; focusing on their good qualities rather than their faults. Remember you can choose your thoughts, so ensure they are productive ones. Sometimes it's helpful to think of saving your energies to fight bigger causes such as injustice in the world, rather than squandering it on petty gossip or self-doubt.

STEP 2: SELF-SOOTHING TECHNIQUES

When you were a child, where did you go for comfort? Our attachment style (see Chapter 2) gives an indication of how we go about this:

➤ Children who feel more or less secure – which is the majority of us – usually go to their mothers, although fathers and other carers also provide a good soothing service. Secure people are able to seek out the comfort of close adults and feel positive about getting social support when they need it.

➤ Ambivalent children want to be soothed but are unsure that their parent-figure is going to do a good enough job. This can lead to clinging and also to cool, distant relationships, as ambivalent attachers never feel they get the distance right; they are either too close or too far apart.

➤ Avoidant attachers don't seek the comfort of their parents and don't readily ask for their needs to be met but appear to be distant and unemotional.

➤ Disorganised attachers, as the name suggests, show features of the other styles and inconsistency in the way they give and receive love and affection.

You may feel that at times you have exhibited some or all of these styles of relating to other people. That's pretty normal. No-one feels secure and in control all of the time. But at Relate we notice how many adults have grown up without learning some useful techniques for soothing *themselves*. We all know about the less-than-useful comforters that seem easy and soothing at the time but can be so destructive: comfort eating, excessive alcohol or drugs, or any other kind of addictive behaviour. And what about those who expect their loved ones to provide all the comforting they need and then are disappointed and angry when they feel they don't get enough help?

So take a moment to think. When you feel low and have those negative, niggling voices ringing in your head, what do you tend to do about it? Reach for a quick fix? Phone a friend? Or are you able to self-soothe and calm yourself down?

Self-soothing techniques don't have to be complicated. You might benefit from a long soak in the bath or making a cup of tea. Enjoying a chat and a laugh with a good friend is a great soother, as is watching a comedy film. Some people swear by sport or physical exercise: half an hour's walk around a park or in a wild, windy spot is a free tonic if you're feeling down. And don't forget to stop negative head chatter by saying 'NO!' (see Step 1).

Sitting on your own, watching the sky and breathing deeply is a sure way of calming down. Take a deep breath in to a count of four, hold it for a count of two and then let it out on a count of six. If you concentrate on your breathing you will dispel anxiety. If you are stuck in an office or traffic, try picturing in your mind a beautiful place, a mountain or flowing water. Some like to create order around them by therapeutic cleaning, organising or gardening. This calms us by creating a feeling of control over our surroundings at moments when we don't feel in charge of the chaos inside our heads.

If you have been keeping a journal and are developing the writing bug, a good self-soothing technique is to write letters and notes to yourself. Alternatively, get friends and colleagues to send letters to you. Basically, this is about 'bigging yourself up' so don't be afraid to stick these notes, drawings or letters up where you will regularly see them, such as on the fridge, above a desk or on a notice board.

PETER (39) *I keep a note from a colleague stuck on my computer, saying: 'I love to work with you. It's fun, relaxed and interesting. I especially appreciate your mischievous sparkle.' It's now faded and yellow with age but just reading that message in someone else's handwriting, saying nice things, makes me feel happy.*

You could write a funny or touching note to any family member, friend or work colleague which will be a real pick-me-up. While you're about it, get them to do the same for you in return. Here is an example of a jokey note that cheered up Syeed:

Dear Syeed

Just a quick note to say how much we in the office value the fantastic contribution you make to this company. We all admire you tremendously, right down to your Arsenal socks and unusual 1980s desert boots. You are a prince among human beings and . . . I love you, man!

Yours sincerely

Dr No (your boss)

Syeed pinned it above his desk and every time he looked at it, he laughed.

Decide on your favourite self-soother and practise it. Write about how you get on in your journal.

STEP 3: IMAGINING A NEW FUTURE

There is something very powerful in this exercise because it clearly focuses attention on what you want to achieve.

You can explore this with a friend, if that would help. Write down in your journal how you would like life to look in six months' time. Try and pack in as much detail as possible:

Home
➤ Would you decorate a room or the whole flat/house?
➤ Could some therapeutic cleaning/organising be satisfying?
➤ Could you get others to help you with these tasks?

Friends
➤ Who do you see in the supportive, loving band of friends around you?

Work
➤ How do you see your job in six months' time?
➤ Would you like to get a job or change jobs?

Love
➤ What would you like your romantic life to look like?
➤ What will your sexual relationship be like?
➤ How will you look when you feel happily in love?

Family
➤ How do you want your relationship with friends, family members and children to be?

Finances
➤ How would you like to feel about your income in six months' time?

As you are doing this reflecting, think and write about it in a positive way. What positive impact would these changes have on your life? Who else, and what else, would be positively affected by the changes? When you feel that you really have captured how you would like your life to be in six months, close your eyes and take some deep breaths and experience your life as you have written it down. Really imagine that you have achieved all that you would like to.

How do you feel? Fantastic I hope. Our thoughts and feelings are like magnets – if you think and imagine more positive thoughts and images, you start to rewrite you life and your life will start improving. What is important is that you keep focusing on the positive. We are much more attractive when we are clear about what we want.

STEP 4: GRATITUDE AND APPRECIATION

The fourth step is to focus on how grateful you are for what you have in this moment – right now. Choose a comfortable chair and close your eyes. Take some deep breaths. Notice how you are feeling safe and comfortable right now and that in this moment you feel fully alive and content. Then cast your mind over the good things in your life: friends, family, children, health, pets, hobbies, or something really small that you are happy about.

Being grateful for the things that we have in our lives already enables us to appreciate life and to find happiness in the simple things in our day-to-day living: enjoying a cup of tea with a delicious slice of cake; reading a good book; spending time with a friend or just enjoying the sunshine. Appreciation is a way of tapping into our happiness. If we feel happier, we are healthier and more attractive to be around, with the added bonus that we feel calmer.

STEP 5: ACCEPTING THE PAST – AND LETTING IT GO

Letting go and forgiving is a powerful process in removing one of the main barriers to finding a loving partner. It allows you to be in the present and to look to the future. Holding you in the past gets you nowhere as your loving partner is in the future.

Write a list in your journal of everyone who has ever done you wrong or upset you: a teacher who was horrible to you at school; an ex-partner; a neighbour who really annoys you. Write it down and, when completed, say to each and every one of them that you have forgiven them – if you wish them well you have forgiven them.

> GINA (50) *I've been swapping text messages with a friend about our ex-partners. We decided to try and write messages of love and gratitude, and it was really difficult for the first 10 days to think of anything good to say! But after 10 days, it became easier to think well of them. It might be hard to believe, but this text-swapping is improving my relationship with my ex.*

While doing this exercise you might find that you need some help to look at deep-seated hurts from the past. You might want to book an appointment with a Relate counsellor to see how they can support you in that process. Another route is to speak to your doctor as GP surgeries often have on-site counsellors who can help or refer you to specialist services.

Another way of soothing the wounds of past relationships that went wrong and starting the process of healing your heart is to write a letter to your ex. Talk in the letter about how you feel and that now you are ready to let go of the past and the hurt you experienced. As you seal the envelope, look to the future and the type of person you want to attract into your life. If it feels right, send the letter. If not, burn it, shred it or do whatever feels right. The action of writing the letter and sealing the envelope will be starting the process of letting go of some of the past and opening up the possibilities of new relationships.

We can never let go of all the hurt from the past but it helps if we forgive the more toxic feelings. Once you've forgiven others, how about focusing that forgiveness on yourself? It's probably long overdue! Maybe even write a letter to yourself. Forgive yourself for remaining in a relationship that was not serving you; reflect on a time when you have been hurt by others and maybe caused hurt to someone. Before you put the letter into the envelope, read it out to yourself and feel the release that you are allowing yourself to have.

MARGARET (52) *I wrote a letter to myself about a relationship that I had which I thought about each day, and every time I thought of it my tummy would tighten and I would get feelings of revenge. After I had followed this process I never thought about the relationship other than in passing. It is truly remarkable.*

STEP 6: SMILE

Now that you are starting to incorporate the positive into your life, you will be feeling happier within yourself. Do you find yourself smiling? The next step on your journey to having a more positive attitude is to smile at everyone you pass as you walk down the street today (as long as it's safe to do so, of course!).

If you can't smile at everyone on the first day, build up to that by smiling at one person at least, and increase the number of people you smile at each day. You will be amazed at the reaction. So many people will smile back at you – yes, even in the UK! If you're at home, smile as you talk on the phone or watch people on television. The very act of smiling makes you and the person you are smiling at feel good. Get into the habit of smiling as you go about your business and you will feel huge benefits.

> *Laughter and smiling are weight-loss for the spirit. The longer I work with people using this material, the more it seems that the fundamental benefit is people simply feel better, 'lighter', for smiling and laughing. It feels good to be alive. The fact that it's also boosting mental, emotional and physical health gives you every reason imaginable to smile and laugh at every opportunity.*

> JOE HOARE, happiness guru

STEP 7: IMAGINE YOUR NEW RELATIONSHIPS

The last step in the programme is to imagine how you want your new relationship or your future husband or wife to be. We don't mean how the other person *looks* (though this might be an important element) but a more general imagining of the kind of people you like, what they like doing and how they make you feel when you're with them. This is quite an unfamiliar thing to think about: usually we just accept our friends and relatives for who they are and don't think about *why* we have chosen them and why they might have chosen us.

In fact, that's a good place to start this step: ask your family and friends what they like about you and what qualities make you an attractive person. You may be surprised by their answers but you could use them as material for writing in your journal about the kind of people you like.

Here are some words that might help:

Happy	Patient	Passionate
Committed	Hard-working	Loving
Kind	Intelligent	Shy
Assertive	Thoughtful	Fun-loving
Steady	Funny	Creative
Genuine	Warm	Relaxed
Sober	Complex	Articulate
Sensitive	Caring	Wild
Sexy	Intense	Tolerant
Dedicated	Traditional	Tender
Self-respecting	Good listener	Easy-going
Consistent	Modest	Supportive
Honest	Sharing	Sensual
Relaxed	Friendly	Encouraging
Mischievous	Calm	Interesting
Wise	Witty	Humble
Quiet	Dramatic	Disciplined

When you start dating, try to remember these positive qualities that you admire in yourself. By working through the plan, we promise you will notice a change in your attitude as it starts to create a virtuous circle of positive thoughts and brings more positivity into your life. In doing this, your experiences with dating, the Internet and relationships will improve and become easier to manage. It's not easy to move from a 'glass half empty' place to a 'glass half full' place, but those who try find it worth the effort and time they put into it.

Are you ready to meet someone yet? If so, let's get going!

Chapter 4

An Active Approach to Finding Love

In our grandparents' day, young single people would have met and married each other – usually with a little plotting from matchmaking aunts – during the course of a fairly predictable and unchanging life. Early marriage and settling down with someone from your own local community would have been expected. Life is much more complex and full of choices today. Many people move some distance from home when they grow up, and we tend to travel more for work and leisure. As a result we are less tied to our communities. In addition, the Internet has influenced the way we socialise, enabling us to connect with other people online rather than having to make the effort to meet face to face.

Against this background of changing family ties and work patterns, a 'love business' has been establishing itself for the last 35 years in the UK and has grown into a multi-million-pound industry. Building on the old idea of the 'matchmaker' who could help shy, workaholic, under-confident or isolated individuals find their perfect partner, the dating scene has now expanded into a huge playground of possibilities, promising love, friendship, a great social life and – most enticing – sex.

The aim of this chapter is to encourage you to take an active approach to finding love. This means finding out what's available to help you then taking the plunge. We'll take an overview of the dating services available and give you tips to help you succeed.

BE PROACTIVE

However keen they are to find someone new, many people think there's something desperate or distasteful about the idea of proactively looking for love. They cling to the idea that 'The One' is going to come walking down their street with Destiny on one side and Fate on the other. They would rather eat their own toes than put themselves out there in a vulnerable place.

If that's the way you feel, we want to change your mind. If you've been sitting around waiting for 'The One' to appear and he/she hasn't arrived yet, then your strategy isn't working, is it? It's time to do something different.

Proactive dating isn't desperate; it's brave and practical. It means making your own agenda, rather than responding to other people's. It means taking hold of what you want in a future love relationship, identifying the barriers to success inside yourself and overcoming them.

If you decide to put an advert in the personal column, join a social group or write a profile for an Internet dating site, you are taking up the reins of the process. You'll decide which people you want to meet, rather than leaving all the decisions to someone else. If you become more courageous in taking opportunities to talk to people and get to know them, that's another example of being proactive. Changing your habits of relating to others can be scary but it does get easier once you have made the decision to be more 'active' in the way you communicate.

DATING SERVICES: AN OVERVIEW

A recent *Which?* survey claimed that six million people in the UK – a large proportion of the single population – now run their romantic lives via the Internet. This makes it the most popular method of meeting new partners, especially among love-seekers under 30. Next in popularity come newspaper advertisement pages, with names like 'soul mates' or 'lonely hearts', where you place written messages about yourself and the sort of person you want to meet.

Introduction agencies promise to interview you personally and find you a certain number of suitable matches. The traditional marriage bureau exists to help the person who wants a third party – an experienced matchmaker – to find them a suitable bride or groom. Finally, there are holidays and social clubs for singles, singles' socialising networks, lunch clubs, speed-dating and chat sites based on hobbies or interests. And let's not forget all the 'traditional' ways of meeting people through friends, leisure or at work.

There are so many opportunities for meeting new people that it pays to look around and decide what suits you best in terms of your personal style, your finances and the amount of spare time you have to devote to it. See Chapters 6 and 7 for more detail on the different types of dating services available.

TIPS FOR SUCCESS

Don't Put All Your Eggs in One Basket

Whichever dating service you choose, the proactive dater starts off by contacting several interesting-looking people at one time. This is because, if you put all your eggs in one basket, you could well be disappointed and it might affect your self-esteem. The idea of contacting several people is not to be selfish or shallow but to increase your confidence in making friends and becoming a good conversationalist. By doing this, you avoid the common pitfall of coming across – and feeling – needy, desperate, anxious, perfectionist or vulnerable (see Michael's case study, below). This strategy of arranging several dates or e-mailing several different people at the same time is particularly good for easing you back into the world of romance in a relaxed way without pinning too much hope on any one relationship.

'I'm No Good at Relationships.' Michael, 29

Michael came to Relate full of anxieties that were stopping him even taking the first step towards meeting someone special.

I start messing up the moment I make a date with a woman. Last week, I hung around outside the café, scared to go inside. I could see this woman, waiting at a table for me, but my palms were sweating. What can she have thought when she saw me scurrying away towards my car? When I got home I was cursing myself, saying I was stupid and worthless. I meant to ring and apologise but couldn't bring myself to do it.

I'm longing for a good relationship, and if only I could get over this stage-fright I'm sure I could get close to someone. My parents are both rather anxious people so I feel there is both nurture and nature in my fears: some of it inherited from my parents and some conditioning from my upbringing. My mother was over-protective, leading to a feeling that the world is an unsafe place.

Michael shows some signs of social anxiety. Anxiety in social situations is the second most common anxiety problem after panic attacks. Michael needs to talk back to the negative voices in his head and to break down some of his irrational thinking about meeting new people. As well as seeing a counsellor, Michael has joined a self-help group so that he can practise holding conversations in a safe space. He has met Kelly, who has become a great supporter and friend. The counsellor has suggested Michael should practise calming himself down by concentrating on his breathing, noticing his breath going in and out.

Michael is learning that he doesn't need to take responsibility for all social occasions. It is enough that he should turn up looking friendly and relaxed. He'd been taking all the burden of ensuring a 'perfect' evening onto his own shoulders, and it was his fear of failing at this task that led to actual failure. Instead of picturing himself chatting to someone over a cup of coffee, Michael's feverish mind would fearfully imagine all sorts of things like getting engaged, married and dumped by this date he'd never met!

Michael still occasionally feels the pull of old behaviour in social situations. Instead of listening to the negative voices saying he's stupid, however, Michael laughs it off. He asks the other person a question, which he finds useful because it diverts him from worrying about his performance. He has developed a deep friendship with Kelly, which they think might turn into something more.

Time Constraints

Consider how many hours you can put aside for romance, and what part of the day suits you best for meetings. Obviously, the time you have available will, to some extent, influence the kind of people you will meet. For example, if you are a single parent who finds it impossible to get out in the evenings, your dating choices will be more limited. Consider your options: could you buddy up with another single parent who also wants a regular evening free for babysitting swaps, or put some effort into finding a trustworthy teenager for regular babysitting? If evenings aren't possible, don't rule out breakfast, coffees, lunchtime or a drink after work.

Ted put all his energies into dating just one woman he met via the Internet. Unfortunately, Jeni lived 70 miles away, which made the time they did spend together feel pressurised. After three Sundays of trekking up and down the M6, Jeni called a halt to things and Ted felt not just disappointed but worn out. He took a few weeks off from dating in order to reconsider his priorities and re-targeted his search on people living within a 15-mile radius of his home.

Work Out Your Budget

Comparing the costs of different dating services before signing up is a good way to match your wallet to your romantic hopes. The costs of services vary considerably:

➤ Free – book groups, supermarket deli counters, matchmaking by friends, art galleries, dog-walking.

➤ Modestly priced – Internet dating, dining clubs, evening classes. Personal ads look cheap but prices can mount up to around £40 per month or £5 per call if you decide to use premium rate telephone numbers (see Chapter 7).

➤ Moderately priced – some introduction services (see Chapter 7).

➤ Pricey – services with a high content of personal help, expertise and advice, such as premium introduction services and marriage bureaus.

If money is tight, it might be a good idea to make a budget before starting your search for love. Don't underestimate the hidden costs of dating, like transport, parking, drinks, meals and socialising, not to mention making yourself look good for those dates: outfit, shoes, haircut, make-up, beauty treatments . . .

Don't Judge People Too Quickly

Some people who are looking for love try to protect themselves by being overly critical or prickly about anyone who comes near. This takes several forms. It could be about status and earnings, as in: 'I won't date anyone who's not a manager or a director.' It could be about looks: 'I won't meet anyone who's shorter than me or a few pounds overweight.' Or it could be about personality: 'I've got to have a partner who's very serious and interested in cars.' We've even heard of those who pick partners according to astrological signs, as in: 'He has to be Sagittarius with Virgo rising.'

It's worth exposing some of these must-haves to a reality test. First of all, think about your own past love relationships. Did those men or women live up to your ideal and perfect standards? Probably not. It's much more likely that when you first met them, you didn't think 'this is The One' but got to know them more gradually and the feelings built naturally over time.

Now think about your friends. Did they choose their wives and husbands by hair colour, profession or just one small aspect of personality? Again, hopefully not. They most likely hitched up because they liked the whole package and became friends, which led to falling in love.

In fact, when people have a checklist based on height, weight, appearance and status, often what they are trying to do is 'clone' a previous relationship of significance: to re-create a girlfriend or boyfriend from a past love affair that went wrong or a marriage that has ended, or even to conjure up the shadow of a partner who has died. These attempts, which are often unconscious, are likely to fail because we're not clones; we're all individuals who ultimately seek the freedom to be ourselves.

So when you catch yourself being too fussy about the details, remember it's shooting yourself in the foot because you're narrowing down the number of people you could get to know. If you like someone's online profile because it's funny and you seem to have a lot in common, but there's one aspect that puts you off – age, status or appearance – then consider the whole package before you make your decision to reject them.

'No-one's Good Enough to Father my Baby.' Anthea, 30s

I've done a lot of dating and met a lot of men since splitting with my husband five years ago. I get one date but then men don't seem to want to meet me again. I don't know why, unless it's because they are just too weak and lifeless that they find me a bit too much. My husband was like that, such a useless failure that he had to go off and have an affair with my best friend.

The agency isn't finding the right men for me. They're mainly not tall enough, not intelligent enough or they don't have careers that I can respect. And when I mention that I would like to be a mother within two years, they sometimes look a bit nervous.

Anthea seems to have a hard shell that makes her come across initially as tough and unlikeable. If she thinks about it from her date's point of view, what would it be like to go on a date and find yourself facing a 'job interview' about your personal life and your future prospects? What would it be like to be treated as a possible 'sperm donor' for her baby rather than a real human being? After being on the receiving end of such an interview in a role-play session with the counsellor, Anthea realised that her behaviour was putting people off.

She was encouraged to lighten up and to face her painful feelings about the end of her marriage. Instead of looking hard and grim, Anthea began to smile and joke more often as she started to regain the balance in her life. She reconnected with a group of old girlfriends who she had let slip during her search for a 'baby father'. She started to see her longing for a child as an expression of her need for affection without judgement, but gradually realised that her own harsh judgements were scaring the pants off any prospective suitor. Putting broodiness on the back burner, Anthea turned her attention to making friends with the opposite sex and got back in touch with Ali, someone she had dated earlier. This time, Anthea took a balanced interest in Ali and he in her. Instead of bombarding him with questions, there was give and take and they had a much more enjoyable evening.

Anthea's challenge has been to let down her guard and stop acting like the chief executive officer of a company who is interviewing a new assistant.

Think About Your Profile

Whether you decide to use online dating or to place an ad in a newspaper, you will need to be able to describe yourself in an attractive, interesting way. There is more advice on writing an Internet profile in Chapter 6, and a personal ad in Chapter 7. However, before you get to that stage it is well worth spending some time thinking about who you are and how you want to sell yourself. To help identify your strengths and weaknesses, work through the following list of qualities, rating yourself on each one. It can be very helpful to get a close friend to help you.

0 = neither, 1 = slightly, 2 = fairly, 3 = very							
Happy	3 2 1 0 1 2 3						Miserable
Hard-working	3 2 1 0 1 2 3						Laid-back
Kind	3 2 1 0 1 2 3						Unkind
Shy	3 2 1 0 1 2 3						Outgoing
Assertive	3 2 1 0 1 2 3						Unassertive
Steady	3 2 1 0 1 2 3						Wild
Genuine	3 2 1 0 1 2 3						Fake
Warm	3 2 1 0 1 2 3						Reserved
Relaxed	3 2 1 0 1 2 3						Tense
Sensitive	3 2 1 0 1 2 3						Insensitive
Tolerant	3 2 1 0 1 2 3						Intolerant
Tender	3 2 1 0 1 2 3						Rough
Good listener	3 2 1 0 1 2 3						Poor listener
Consistent	3 2 1 0 1 2 3						Inconsistent
Sociable	3 2 1 0 1 2 3						Unsociable
Witty	3 2 1 0 1 2 3						Serious
Quiet	3 2 1 0 1 2 3						Noisy
Gentle	3 2 1 0 1 2 3						Dominant

Afterwards, think about your perceptions and add anything the quiz has left out. Concentrate on the positives: what do you like most about yourself, and why? You could also, perhaps, learn something from the not-so-positives.

Be a Smooth Operator

Most of us don't think about our answerphone message because we never ring our own phones and listen to ourselves. However, when you are starting to meet new people through the Internet, introduction agencies or 'soul mate' ads, you should take a cool, neutral look at what your answering machine is saying about you.

When you decide to ring a potential date or they decide to ring you, the relationship steps up a gear. You will both be listening out for those little nuances and details that the other person's voice gives away about them. Is your answerphone the aural equivalent of a Siberian winter, making you sound like you are hibernating under six feet of snow? Were you so intimidated by setting up your answerphone message that you ended up sounding fed-up, flat, dull, tired, desperate, bored or bad-tempered? Or does your outgoing message sound like someone you'd want to meet – relaxed, confident, fun, warm and welcoming? Now's the time to check the device is working properly and is giving out a positive message.

TONI (33) *I was on the point of leaving the dating scene when I read about Mal in a local listings magazine. He'd travelled, I'm not interested in travel. To my eyes, he didn't have a very interesting written profile. But when we spoke on the phone there was this quality to him of gentleness, kindness and energy. And I knew as soon as we met that I wanted to be with him.*

Be Cautious

Although it is flattering to get lots of replies to a personal ad or Internet profile, and you may be surprised by dozens of men wanting to chat to you online or meet up with you in person, make sure you do a sift and think carefully before hitting the reply button or answering any phone calls. You can eliminate e-mails or letters that don't refer to you or your profile which are posted by people who answer hundreds of adverts compulsively. (This is not a problem with recorded phone messages as the cost of all those premium telephone calls puts them off.) Also, sift out those who write long, rambling replies with pictures of their Porsches/aeroplanes/space vehicles. You may have been brought up politely but now's the time to let go of your nice manners. It is perfectly acceptable to ignore messages that are rude, hastily typed, inappropriately sexual or just plain bizarre!

If you reply to a personal ad, take a bit of time to get to know the person on the phone before meeting. Don't give out your home phone number; stick to a mobile. You can pick up a lot of information from someone's voice, and if you don't like what you hear, be ready to give a reason for not meeting, honest or otherwise. Your safety is more important than a date with a stranger, so don't give your surname, home or work phone number or address to anyone until you are ready to meet.

Be Organised

Once you have sifted through the replies to your ad, hopefully you will be left with a list of PPM (Possible Partner Material). Get out your journal and give half a page to each person, making notes about their interests and where you contacted them. It's very easy to lose track when you have a dozen or more possible dates.

Some groups of romance-seekers face particular challenges when it comes to finding a partner. In the next chapter, we look at the situation for separated, divorced and widowed people; people over 55; and gay and lesbian daters.

Chapter 5

Dating with Your Needs in Mind

This chapter gives advice for people with specific dating needs:

➤ People who have been separated, divorced or widowed

➤ People over 55

➤ Gay and lesbian daters

DATING AFTER SEPARATION OR DIVORCE

When you separate or divorce, it inevitably has an effect on your social life and your friendships. However much your friends say that they won't take sides and want to stay friends with both of you, it's very difficult to do that. Separating partners usually need to avoid each other. They don't wish to go to the same dinners, the same pubs or the same parties. In order to help them keep apart from each other, friends of the couple have to juggle. This is difficult and they find themselves staying closer to one person than the other.

Friends feel awkward when you split because it's like a bereavement for them as well as for you: they are sad about the couple or family they knew which doesn't exist any more. They don't know what to say and often end up saying nothing at all. Your separation or divorce may be seen as threatening – if it can happen to you, it can happen to them too. Indeed, as a single man or woman again among a crowd of couples, you may be perceived by friends as a threat to their marriage. Friends don't know how to behave around the couple who are splitting and may act as if a break-up or divorce is a disease that is 'catching'.

Children and both sets of families can get caught in this awkwardness too. Although many family members and friends will go out of their way to be kind to your children if they know a split has happened, others will feel torn loyalties, and this could result in fewer social invitations. Some adults or children may feel angry towards a partner who's had an affair or they feel has behaved badly, leading to further distancing from your family. As Sonia says: 'I feel badly for my children that they no longer see their cousins because that part of the family sided with my ex. It doesn't seem fair on any of the children but there's nothing we can do.' All this can be upsetting. At a time when you might be feeling raw, vulnerable and in need of friends, some of them won't be around and available.

However, you have to keep believing that things will improve and that there is someone out there who's right for you. If you tell people what you need from them, you will always find someone who will support you through tough moments and help you get back on your feet. Have a look at pages 73–4 for more about coping with feelings of loss or grief. See page 150–54 for more thoughts about how to minimise the disruption to children and the wider family and how to gather support around your new partner and second family.

DATING AFTER BEREAVEMENT

If you feel you are still grieving the loss of your partner, put off the search for new love until you feel stronger and more positive. It is often said that the process of grieving, which varies greatly between individuals, means that it can take between one and two years before you feel ready to face the world again. You could think about getting some bereavement counselling with Relate or Cruse, the organisation for widows and widowers. At the end of this book are details of some websites where bereaved people can support each other. The anonymity and privacy offered by the Internet can be very helpful to many who are grieving.

If you have been widowed, it can seem daunting to be contemplating finding another partner. One way around this is to concentrate on 'meeting new people' rather than thinking about 'finding a new husband or wife'. If you are traditionally minded, this might be unfamiliar thinking, but it works because it helps you feel more approachable and relaxed about meeting people.

If you do feel nervous, boost your self-confidence before you start looking by following the steps in our Positivity Plan (see Chapter 3). Confide in a trusted friend – perhaps he or she would also like to meet new people and you could be buddies for each other?

'I Made Myself Look Forward to the Future Again.' Ellen, 30s

Ellen was widowed suddenly in her 30s, at a time when she and her husband had been planning their future family. It was the hardest thing in the world for her to think of the future at a time of great sorrow. But Ellen found that committing herself to one or two small, regular steps of hope could go alongside grieving fully for the loss she had experienced:

This is how I approached the 'dating thing' after my husband died when I was still grief-wrenched, lonely and aware that I had to get on with things if I wanted a chance to have my own kids.

I made a list (actually a small drawing) of all the things that made my heart sing that I could still do (playing with friends' kids, dancing, walking). I made sure I did one of them every day so that I didn't let my life be consumed by either grief for the old or yearning for the new.

I used affirmations. Mine went something like: 'I know how to be happy and, at the right time, I will meet someone I can be happy with, and somehow or other we will create a loving family.' This was a lot better than lying in bed working out how many years, then months, weeks, days, hours, minutes (my maths always broke down at this point) I was going to have to live my unhappy life without Ben (assuming death aged 96 as per my grandma's).

In due course, Ellen did meet a lovely man she was able to start a family with.

THE OLDER DATER

Older folk don't want to be thought of as older folk. They see themselves as the liberated generation – free, unburdened and ready for adventure. It may be a marketing agency's dream but many mature daters know that 60 is the new 40, 70 is the new 50 and, for all I know, 80 the new 60! Whatever your years, age is no barrier to finding new love and companionship. Grey power is growing: by the year

2030 there are predicted to be more than 1.3 million people over 90 in the UK population.

There are plenty of ways to increase your circle of friends and meet the kind of people you like:

➤ Search through your address book and phone people you haven't spoken to in years. Most people like to get a phone call but it's easy to get out of the habit of being sociable.

➤ Ask your relatives and friends to think of single people who might like to meet you. Nothing ventured, nothing gained, and they will admire your *chutzpah* for asking!

➤ Think about what you love doing, be it gardening, days out or reading books, and join a group or local course so you can do that activity with like-minded people. The University of the Third Age (www.u3a.org.uk) helps people over 55 to gain new skills. This is a great place to start and costs just a few pounds a year to join because members share their skills with each other rather than paying for tutors. If you are able to access the Internet, the U3A runs 'virtual' or online groups which are useful for those who live in isolated places or find it harder to get out and about.

➤ Your local librarian, Age Concern or local authority might be able to suggest other groups that would be stimulating and where you'd meet like-minded people, such as Workers' Educational Authority networks. Local councils often provide free or very low-cost courses, groups and facilities.

➤ If you live in sheltered housing or have a community of friends nearby, there's nothing to stop you making a group booking at a theatre or a coach booking for a day trip and getting a discount.

Outdated ideas about courtship can be the older person's worst enemy when it comes to new love. Remember that women can ask men out these days; it doesn't have to be the other way round! Try being daring: when you see someone you like, invite them round for coffee along with a small group of friends; this should stop the atmosphere from feeling forced or overwhelming. If you can plan to sit next to them, you can find out more about them in a relaxed environment.

The Internet has shrunk the world and brought it into our living rooms. Older romance-seekers may be surprised by the variety of online agencies, chat rooms and organisations designed to bring older people together. A significant proportion of 'silver surfers' have personal Internet access or can access a computer via community rooms or libraries. If you don't use the Internet but would like to learn, contact your local library for details of free courses.

If you use a search engine and enter words like 'older', 'mature', 'dating' and 'UK', up will pop a large number of sites especially for love-seekers over 55. Some companies that run dating services for all age groups will have particular services dedicated to mature clients. Other Internet dating sites also run a personal introduction agency where you travel to an office for an interview with a 'matchmaker' who takes into account your interests and preferences and promises to find you a certain number of dates over a six-month or twelve-month period. (See Chapter 6 for more information on online dating.)

Among the opportunities for placing or answering personal ads, *Saga* magazine stands out with its lively romance-seekers column, while *The Lady* is a more traditional magazine which contains ads for companions.

WHERE ARE THE MATURE MEN?

The biggest challenge for women over 55 is to attract men back into romance. Older men may feel they don't have the skills to find another partner, or worry that it might be upsetting to the memory of their late partner. Mature women tend to have better social skills and be more flexible in their requirements of a new friendship.

Often it's a long time since either party faced the challenges associated with courtship. Dating experts say that men in mature age groups may not know how to have a friendship without sex so can appear rather insensitive if the woman doesn't immediately want to get into a sexual relationship. This can result in women having a rather low opinion of men or in men looking for a 'younger model'.

Agencies that match mature daters report that men frequently want to recapture their youth by getting attached to a much younger partner. These age-imbalanced relationships are sometimes driven by a search for financial and emotional security by the woman. However, as we often see at Relate, large age differences that seem unimportant in the first excitement of meeting a new partner can cause great tensions later on because each partner is at a different life stage; for example, one partner is retired while the other is still at the height of their career.

DAPHNE (70) *After two years of grieving for my husband's death, I put a lot of energy into meeting new people, via friends, a dating agency with a social club attached to it and now I'm on the Internet. To be honest, there aren't enough available men and I feel I am competing with younger women. I've been on three dates and all of them were pleasant. I was surprised when the gentlemen didn't call back even when they said they would – it seemed impolite, somehow. I also met a man who seemed to want a housekeeper and right away wanted to know when I could move in. That put me off – I have no intention of living with someone again, especially not as a housekeeper! But it's early days so fingers crossed.*

It might be a hangover from earlier decades when it was regarded as rude to ask a person's age, but mature daters seem to be cagey about how old they are. It's an issue that comes up, time and again, among romance-seekers over 50. You'll notice in the personal ads that men seem to want to date women younger than themselves, while women tend to either have no preference regarding age or seek someone around their own age. This difference in expectations contributes to the apparent shortage of men in the over-50s age group. It is socially sanctioned for men to date younger women – the extreme example of this is the 'trophy wife' – but it's getting more common for older women to date considerably younger men.

The main complaint among mature daters is of those who lie about their age. You can fib about your age on an e-mail or in an advert but it's not a good start to a relationship if someone looks you in the eye and claims to be a lot younger than they are. They may look younger and they may act younger, but the lack of honesty may cause doubts to form in the date's mind.

John, 54, was taken with Mandy's profile and they seemed to have the same love of travelling in Greece. In fact, they got on really well when they met in person. John found Mandy to be charming and youthfully attractive. However, she confessed over dinner that she was not 49 but, in fact, was going to be 61 next birthday. Despite their obvious compatibility, John felt he would never consider settling down with a woman older than himself. He didn't know why, but he felt strongly about it, and thought if she was willing to lie about this, what else might she be dishonest about? They never did get to see the Greek islands together.

SEX IN LATER LIFE

Making love with a new partner can be wonderful and just the thing to keep both people feeling young and alive. Lovemaking doesn't have to be about swinging from the chandeliers (though don't let anyone stop you!); it can be about tenderness and companionship as well as passion. In the end, it's about what feels right for you as an individual and as a couple.

Don't let a lack of confidence about your body put you off. Take a light-hearted approach – remove the spectacles and turn the lights down low – and just go with the flow. But if you feel you don't want to have sex, it's not obligatory. Lots of mature relationships are platonic, built on companionship and shared interests. Don't forget that older men may worry about their ability to hold an erection or their attractiveness just as much as women may worry about the loss of a good figure.

PROS AND CONS OF MATURE DATING

Here are some advantages of a new relationship later in life:

➤ The chance to find love, sex and companionship again. 'I may be 74, but I feel like 24!'

➤ Sociability. 'I feel happier and less lonely with a partner.'

➤ He knows you already. 'Reconnecting with someone I first knew when I was 18 makes me feel young again.'

➤ Shared memories. 'He remembers my mother and father. We love reminiscing about the old neighbourhood where we lived.'

➤ Male companion. 'It's lovely to feel protected by a man who can look after travel arrangements and lend you an arm.'

➤ Best of both worlds. 'We each have our own flat and don't want to live together.'

➤ Help with living. 'I do the DIY and she does the cooking. It suits us both.'

➤ Financial support. 'Pooling our resources means we're much better off.'

➤ Family benefits. 'We've both expanded our network by getting to know the other's children and grandchildren.'

➤ Health. 'We can look after the other if one of us feels unwell.'

And here are a few disadvantages:

➤ Compromise. 'It's hard to compromise after all these years of being independent.'

➤ Loyalty. 'Would it be disloyal to the memory of my wife if I married again?'

➤ Fear. 'I couldn't go through the pain of losing another partner.' 'I'm concerned about what will happen if one of us gets ill.'

➤ Confidence. 'At my age, I don't think anyone will want me.'

➤ Stuck in patterns. 'He's very rigid about everything. We can't go out on Thursdays because he has to organise the garage.'

➤ Loss of freedom. 'I've got used to pleasing myself about where I go and how I behave.'

➤ Finances. 'My children are concerned about my lady friend inheriting my property, which is going to cause bad feeling.'

➤ Families. 'We spend a lot of time with her family and I don't particularly like them.'

➤ Sex. 'I'm worried that he'll look for a younger model and won't fancy me.'

➤ Sex, again. 'At my age, I don't want to have sex!'

➤ Libido. 'She wants to make love regularly but I'm not up to it.'

➤ Chores. 'He expects me to do all the cooking now.'

Spend some time writing about what you want from a new relationship, adding some pros and cons from your own experience, before deciding on your strategy for getting to know some interesting new people.

GAY AND LESBIAN DATING

The dating scene for gay men and women is very different from just a few years ago. This is thanks to the increased visibility and acceptability of gay relationships and, of course, the Internet. While meeting and dating someone of the same sex used to involve secret code words and covert liaisons, today's gay singles are more open than ever about where and how to find their perfect partner.

If gay bars and clubs are not your scene – and for many people they aren't – there are plenty of other ways to seek out and meet a same-sex partner. Most of the UK's larger cities have a Gay and Lesbian Switchboard – the number will be in the phone book – which can give you information on local social groups and events. These provide opportunities to meet other gay and lesbian people in a relaxed setting, such as film nights and book groups, or one-offs, like bonfire night fireworks or Halloween parties. Social networking sites are another way of finding out about local events and making friends. Some operate for men only; others for women, or both sexes.

GAY ONLINE DATING

For men looking to meet someone online, there are dozens of gay dating sites available. All have thousands of men registered with photos and profiles, so picking someone who fits your criteria is easy. Some of these sites have an international membership, making it as simple to fix up a date during a trip abroad as in your local area. The downside of these sites, however, is that they tend to be used for 'hook-ups' rather than anything more permanent, so if you're after a long-term partner, you may be disappointed. Some users might also be frustrated by the number of straight men registered who are simply looking for gay sex outside an existing relationship.

Similar sites also exist for women, but in the main, the online lesbian dating scene is a lot more serious-minded. One of the largest, an international site with a membership of 75,000 across the world and 14,000 in the UK, is clearly aimed at women looking for a lasting relationship. The registration process asks you to post a detailed profile as well as a photo, allowing you to find out a lot about a prospective partner before getting in touch. The standard questions that form the basis of the profile even include the question 'Are you willing to relocate?' – this gives a flavour of what the site is hoping to achieve. There are also several pages devoted to stories of women who have met through the site and are now happily living together or married.

Bisexual women or men have a choice of gay or straight dating sites as virtually all straight sites offer the option of dating both men and women. All you have to do is say who you are and whether you're looking for a man or a woman or either: nowhere in the process do you need to define yourself as gay or lesbian. Although these general sites are aimed primarily at the straight market and therefore only a small percentage of advertisers may be looking for a gay relationship, they are valuable because of the sheer number of people listed. They are also a good option for those who feel at all uncomfortable with visiting a specifically gay site. Most of these sites have a subscription fee for 3, 6 or 12 months, but you'll often be able to use the site for free for a short period. Some large sites are free to users and make their money from advertising.

It's worth noting that all the sites mentioned, not just those for gay men and lesbians, are restricted to those aged 18 and over.

GAY PERSONAL ADS

The personal ads listed in many national newspapers and magazines have sections for 'men seeking men' and 'women seeking women'. Virtually all of these personal columns are now available online as well as in the pages of the newspapers. Most ads give a voicebox number, which you call to hear a recorded message (while paying for a premium rate number). Being able to hear a prospective partner's voice is often the best way of knowing whether or not you want to meet.

SANDRA (33) *I met my partner online, after a long period of being single and not knowing where to meet other lesbians. After exchanging e-mails with probably a dozen women, I started a serious correspondence with Janice. We e-mailed for a couple of months before I decided to go up to Scotland to meet her. We hit it off from the moment we met. She is the most amazing woman: kind, successful and beautiful as well! We are now moving into our own flat and are planning to get married sometime next year.*

In the next chapter, we look in more detail at Internet dating which, over the last decade, has become the UK's most popular way to find a partner.

Chapter 6

Internet Dating

Around six million Britons admit to using the Internet to find a partner. In a 2009 survey of 1,500 online dating websites for the magazine *Which?*, 71 per cent of users said they had been on a date, or knew someone who had been on a date, with someone they'd met through an online dating site. One in six had found a long-term relationship as a result of online dating.

Online dating is now a mainstream activity and there's no stigma left to finding a partner via the Internet. The immediacy and anonymity of the Internet also means that more and more men are being attracted to finding love in cyberspace. People from 18 to 80 are signing up to chat and meet people. There are sites to suit all tastes and interests, such as vegetarian daters, plump partners, posh partners, holiday buddies and eco-friendly daters. Dating agencies operate within faith communities for Christians, Jewish people and Muslims. In fact, new sites for bringing people together seem to be springing up all the time.

JASMINE (38) *After four years of gathering courage I tried Internet dating. I met three people through one free site and then moved to its sister, paid-for site, where I met about 15 people and chatted online to another 30. I have been on 60 dates in the last six months and met some really great people.*

HOW DOES ONLINE DATING WORK?

Joining an online dating site is different to joining an introduction agency because members do not undergo background checks or have any personal contact with online dating site staff. Instead, you register with a website in the comfort of your own home and create an online dating profile page by writing about yourself and uploading photographs, and even videos, of yourself for others to view. Users can then browse other online dating profiles to find someone they like, or search for suitable dates using key words, location or criteria such as age range, religion, height or hobbies. Many online dating sites sell other services such as lunch clubs and holidays as well as acting like an introduction agency by sifting and recommending potential matches to you through a computerised system of selection known as the 'lists method'. The list can be posted or e-mailed to you after payment of a fee.

SIGNING UP TO AN ONLINE DATING SITE

Most online dating agencies allow new members to register and set up an online dating profile free of charge. They charge a subscription fee for full website functionality or certain important features, such as tools for communicating with other members.

Online dating package prices vary considerably depending on how many months' membership you purchase in one go or sign up for in advance. As a guide, a month's online dating membership typically costs between £10 and £25, though many sites offer daily, weekly, six-monthly or annual package deals which offer bigger discounts the longer your subscription. There's also a growing number of free online dating services that generally work like social networking sites as a place to 'meet' people. These sites do not charge for access or use of features; instead, they make money through displaying advertising.

Don't blow your budget by signing up to loads of different dating sites on a whim. It's tempting to get out the credit card in order to see if there's anyone just around the corner or newly signed up to a site, but that's an expensive way of meeting people. Also, if you join too many sites at once you may feel overwhelmed and end up using none of them.

If you check out some of the different Internet dating sites without joining up, you will notice that they offer different functions. For example, one will offer an up-front opportunity to date *either* UK men or women or *both*, recognising that a significant proportion of their clientele is gay, bisexual or 'bi-curious'. Another might be an international site where the majority of clients seem to be looking for partners in another country. Spend some time looking at what's on offer before deciding upon a site that looks right for you.

WRITING YOUR ONLINE PROFILE

Your online dating profile page features your responses to set questions about your hobbies, preferences and interests, along with photos and a self-written character description. It's this written description that many people find the most daunting aspect of online dating. After all, how do you sum yourself up in just a couple of hundred words?

It's surprising how many searchers seem to put minimal effort into writing their profile. You'd have to ask yourself whether the authors of these profiles are shy, new to this activity or simply not interested enough in meeting someone. The least successful profiles are extremely short and scrappy, saying things like: 'Don't know what to write, just need a man.' To many readers, that message comes across off-puttingly as: 'I'm desperate and haven't got any hobbies, interests or friends of my own.'

Spell-check the text before you post it, and reread it to make sure it'll make sense to people who don't know you. Your profile could potentially be read by hundreds of other users, so avoid inappropriate jokes or language. Stay safe by not volunteering any personal information such as your address, employer's name or contact details. Here are some further tips:

Be Honest

Don't pretend to be someone you're not. Expand on the answers you gave to any preset questions when you signed up to the site. If you are a busy parent or a workaholic, say so. Think about your good points and don't be negative or needy. Be specific about your interests in order to tempt people to contact you: talk about your holiday, your dog, your fascination with caravans, anything that makes you seem interesting and different. If you are a single parent, your life may revolve around your lovely children but try to concentrate on yourself for a few minutes and remember all the things you are interested in outside your kids. Never talk about your ex-partner or why your last relationship ended.

Say What You are Looking For

There are likely to be hundreds of eligible members that fit key criteria such as age and location. This is your chance to whittle out the ones that will not be suitable. What will make your ideal partner different from the rest? If there's an important area of your life that a new partner would have to fit in with – such as your children – then say so. It'll save time in the long run, and ultimately improve your chances of success.

Browse Other Profiles

Browse other people's online dating profiles and make a note of what attracts you or puts you off. Write down the things you'd want to know before getting in touch with a potential date. The chances are you'll have these elements in common with people who'd potentially like to meet you. Look at what people's online names say about them. You'll notice that names like Fastlove or Boobylicious suggest that the author is looking for sex, and the replies will assume that's all they want. Make sure your online name reflects something about your personality and your hopes for romance.

Each profile you look at will have a word that describes what sort of relationship the author is looking for. These will be words like 'fun', 'random play only', 'friendship', 'fun and sex', 'relationship', 'travel companion' and 'serious relationship'. If you choose someone who has specified fun, random play or fun and sex, you are choosing someone who is saying clearly that they do not want a committed relationship.

Most sites will allow you to have a quick look at the last 50 or 100 people who signed up. You will quickly spot the profiles that are going to be popular – in fact, some sites even rank profiles in order of popularity so you can see what those people are doing right.

Ask For a Friend's Opinion

Ask a close friend to give you some feedback on what they think are your defining characteristics. Ask what their most enduring memories of you are or how they'd describe you to someone you've never met. There is at least one site where you can get your friend to write your profile on your behalf.

CHOOSING A PHOTO FOR YOUR PROFILE

They say a good picture is worth a thousand clicks. In fact, some online dating websites estimate that profiles with a photo get up to 15 times more attention than those without.

Be Honest

Take the same approach to choosing your picture as you do to writing your online profile (see page 90). Choose a recent snap that is neither too honest nor too flattering. Your picture should clearly show your face, be properly focused and in colour. If you can put up more than one photo, do so, including one head and shoulders photo and a full-length shot. Never be tempted to post a flattering photo of yourself taken some years ago when you were thinner and younger as it leads to awkwardness on both sides when you meet in person. Men and women are both guilty of choosing over-flattering photos but, in the long run, it's not worth the hassle.

Show Your Personality

Give some clues to your personality by selecting a photo taken in a setting that means a lot to you. If you're a keen traveller or have an interesting hobby, choose a picture that shows you in your element. Expressions and clothing say a lot about people, so pick a photo that captures you enjoying life and dressed to impress. Keep it natural, though; if you usually dress casually don't use a photo of you wearing a hat at a church wedding. Also, don't choose a group shot showing other people, such as ex-partners or children.

> MARTY (48) *A dating disaster would be when the photo looks good and the profile looks interesting and then you find she's aged greatly since the photo was taken or put on a lot of weight. I have found myself feeling sorry for my dates once or twice and agreeing to meet them again and then changing my mind afterwards.*

WEBMAIL

When signing up to an online dating site, you'll be allocated an online e-mail inbox allowing you to send and receive e-mails when on the site. Your webmail e-mails won't go to your personal e-mail inbox (such as a Hotmail or Yahoo account), but you can usually opt to receive e-mail notifications alerting you when a new webmail message is received. All sites offer webmail as the default way of communicating with other online dating site users. Your online dating webmail account will usually be accessible through the 'My messages' area of the website.

INSTANT MESSAGING

Instant messaging, also shortened to IM, enables you to exchange short messages with other online dating site users in real time. If another member is online at the same time as you and you'd like to get in touch, their profile will show an instant messaging prompt that will open up a new window. You then just type in a message and wait for a response.

CHAT

Similar to instant messaging, online chat enables you to exchange messages with other online dating site users in real time. The difference is that online chat takes place in an established area of the website (known as a chat room), and you join existing conversations with multiple or single online daters. Some online dating chat rooms have a preset topic of conversation, while others allow new topics to be set up by members. If you're new to this idea, sit and read what others write for a while before attempting to join in.

VIDEO MESSAGING

If you have a web camera (a webcam) and your dating site offers video messaging, you can send or accept invitations to have live chats with other site members. A key advantage of video messaging is it mimics the experience of face-to-face dating, but in a more secure environment. You also get to see and speak to potential dates to get a better idea of whether you like the look of them. The disadvantage comes if you are not naturally telegenic and may do yourself more harm than good by coming across awkwardly. At the time of writing, few UK sites offer the webcam function so it's unlikely to be a problem.

> MARK (32) *In my Internet profile, I try to be honest about what I'm looking for as it saves me a lot of hassle down the line. I always say I want to meet women who are on a spiritual journey like myself, and people seem to find that makes me a bit different and unconventional. I also say I'm not interested in another live-in relationship so as to try and avoid all those women who are.*

WINKS, POKES, VIRTUAL ROSES AND OTHER FLIRTING

If you read an online profile, look at the pictures and decide you'd like to get to know him or her better, there is a neat way of signalling this. Many sites allow you to send a 'wink' or a 'poke', a message that declares a flirty interest. The person at the other end of the wink can look up your profile and pictures and decide whether or not to 'wink back'.

Winking or, on some sites, sending a virtual rose, a smile or an e-card, is a gentle way of saying 'you look interesting' without exposing yourself too much. And it's good for you proactive daters out there who can wink at loads of people at the same time without feeling guilty. Bear in mind, though, that however flattering it may be to get bombarded by winks and e-mails, you need to evaluate your replies with a healthy scepticism. Learn to read between the lines of what people say.

JASMINE (32) *Within a couple of hours of posting my photograph, I'd received 42 e-mails and winks. By the evening, there were 120 messages in my inbox. It was crazy. It went to my head!*

SHARED INTEREST AND HOBBY CHAT ROOMS

Internet dating websites can be a slightly frightening place for those who just want to 'dip a toe in the water' rather than sign up immediately. The Internet can also be used in a gentler way as a first point of contact with people who have the same hobbies or interests as you do. Whether it's horse-racing, creative writing, recipes or bingo that floats your boat, there will be dozens of chat rooms set up to explore your particular pastime. Whatever the shared hobby or passion, it seems to break the ice and provide a natural and unforced focus for interesting chat. Relationships have a chance to develop more naturally in these places, away from the speed and pressure of the Internet dating scene.

You can choose to talk to others virtually in cyberspace, by instant messaging or via a webcam, if you have one. If you don't have a personal computer, your local library or Internet café provides a chance to get online at low or no cost. After getting to know some of the other members a bit better over a period of months, you might choose to meet up in person, either one-to-one or in a group.

PATRICE (38) *For the past five years I've belonged to a site for creative writers. By reviewing other people's work and chatting about films and books, I have made a regular gang of online friends from all over the world and have met up in person with around 20 of them. Our shared love of reading and films means that we always have something in common. In fact, I know three couples who have married as a result of this website.*

WHAT IF I'M NOT GETTING THE RIGHT KINDS OF REPLIES?

If you're not getting replies from the kind of people you like, sit and review your profile and the sites you have signed up to. It could be that the site is the wrong one for you, or perhaps something in your profile is sending out the wrong signal. Get a friend to check your profile and your photo to see if it gives out the wrong message or signals. Don't forget that a poor photo, bad grammar or spelling or a really scrappy profile are real turn-offs for many people.

Try signing up with several different free sites and compare the kinds of responses you get from each. Some love-seekers use free sites as a place to get their confidence up and to hone their chatting skills but never come across anyone they want to meet. Then, they join a more 'exclusive', paid-for site where they come across like-minded people who are more serious about meeting a new partner. (See also the section on cyberspace and sex, pages 161–65.)

Although online dating has a high success rate, it's not for the faint-hearted and it's not for everybody. Many people will prefer to look at other ways to meet new people, which we cover in the next chapter.

Chapter 7

Agencies, Personals and Other Ways to Meet

If online dating isn't for you, there are many other dating services available to choose from. This chapter looks at introduction agencies, personal ads in newspapers and magazines, and other ideas for ways to meet new people.

INTRODUCTION AGENCIES

There are about 1,000 introduction agencies operating in the UK. New ones, catering for niche markets, are springing up all the time. These agencies tend to be suitable for people who are serious about getting married or are seeking a committed relationship. They are a good option for people who are too busy to manage their own search for a partner. Others prefer to work with an agency because they have been put off by the speed and casualness of the online dating scene.

At a personal interview in their offices, you will be given a form to fill in about your hobbies, occupation, qualifications and income. You will be matched with others on the agency's books according to your stated preferences and theirs. So if you are looking for a tall man living in Manchester with a university degree and a sense of humour, they should be able to give you details of all the men on their books who fulfil those criteria. You may be shown photographs of them and be able to read their profiles.

You might get a fixed number of matches – often six – or an unlimited number. These might be shown to you during your one-to-one interview, or you could be sent a list afterwards. If they cannot find good enough matches to fit your requirements, reputable agencies will not take you onto their books.

The big advantage of a personal interview with a reputable agency is that they will be realistic with you about your hopes and dreams. A good agency interviewer may be more honest than your friends would be. If you are just an ordinary-looking man or woman who is hoping to be hooked up with an Angelina Jolie or a George Clooney, an agency may be able to bring you down to earth and admit that their fantastic-looking clients will have their pick of the crop while the rest of us have to be a little more realistic.

They will tell you whether they have suitable people to match you with. This is a crucial point: try and find out just how many members they have living in your immediate locality. Not all agencies are scrupulous about this as they are trying to earn a living and don't want to turn customers away. But it may well be that your agency has no suitable matches within 100 miles of your house – and that could be a problem.

The best agencies should be honest and sensitive enough to tell you if they think you have a psychological barrier to finding love. It could be that you're not ready to date again, or that they can see you need some help with confidence and assertiveness before embarking on a search for a partner. Some introduction agencies even offer ongoing services with a psychologist or flirt coach who will identify your dating problems and help you to solve them.

For example, let's say you have recently separated from a husband or wife of many years and are not ready to move on. Perhaps you are still grieving the loss of that last relationship or are trying to find a 'copy' of your last partner. A good interviewer will gently suggest giving yourself a bit of space and time, or perhaps recommend looking for 'friendship only' and not trying to make another relationship right away.

Agencies work better for men than for women because most agencies have far more women on their books than men. However, some introduction agencies compensate for this by running Internet sites as well as the agency business and 'poach' the interesting-looking men to introduce to their female customers.

HOW MUCH WILL IT COST?

Costs vary widely – from around £100 to many thousands:

➤ At one large national introduction agency, the standard service costs about £130 for 12 months. This includes three matches by computer on the basis of a questionnaire filled in by the client. Extra matches cost £10 for three.

➤ Another reputable agency offers a personal service costing between £1,000 and £3,000.

➤ A prestige marriage bureau places personal adverts on your behalf, followed by a bespoke matching service where all prospective partners are thoroughly checked, for just under £10,000.

➤ You can pay up to £15,000 as a one-off payment for matchmaking at the most expensive agencies, which seem to act like traditional marriage bureaus for wealthy people.

➤ Another service for 'professional people', in which each client is verified by means of a home visit and an accurate profile is written on the client's behalf by the interviewer, costs about £400 per annum plus £15 per month after the first month.

➤ Dining club membership is often free and each dinner event costs around £35 to £60, or a little more in London.

➤ Agencies catering for specific communities, such as Jews and Muslims, or people with niche interests, are often more affordable.

Reputable agencies are supposed to post their costs on their websites and brochures. If you have to make a call to establish costs, beware of one or two businesses using a hard-sell approach. Don't give details out about yourself – your name, telephone number, address or e-mail – until you're sure you want to buy that service or you could be pestered and find yourself receiving some unwelcome and unwanted mail.

If possible, join an agency that belongs to the umbrella body, the Association of British Introduction Agencies. ABIA represents only a small fraction of the dating agencies operating in the UK and, although there are good agencies that don't belong to ABIA, it does offer standards and protection for the client. For example, if your agency goes bust, you may be taken on by another company.

ABIA agencies must explain the criteria by which they are making matches. The services offered and fees charged must be clearly explained before you part with any cash. Refunds are offered if the agency fails to provide the client with the agreed number of matches. There is a proper process in the event of complaints about the service, and you may get your money refunded if your complaint is upheld.

QUESTIONS TO ASK

Here are some questions you should ask an introduction agency before you sign up:

➤ How many men/women do they have in your age group? Bear in mind that women over 50 and men in their early 20s are the hardest to match in terms of the numbers of suitable partners likely to be on the agency's books.

➤ Does the agency cover your geographical area? They might not have enough clients in your part of the country.

➤ What sort of clients do they attract? What percentage of members comes from a similar educational and social background to yourself?

➤ Does the firm offer a trial membership? Will they put your membership on hold at no extra cost?

➤ What happens if they don't have enough suitable matches? Will you get a refund?

➤ Where do they advertise? Look at the top shelf in the newsagent's. You might not want to join an agency that advertises in girlie magazines.

➤ What is their policy regarding clients who are married or separated?

➤ What method do they use for matching clients?

➤ How will complaints be dealt with?

Don't use agencies that only give a box number and no name and address. They are invariably cons. If you possibly can, visit the offices to see if you like the look of the firm and its staff.

NEWSPAPER AND MAGAZINE ADS

In 1727, Miss Helen Morrison, described as a 'lonely spinster', became the first woman to place a lonely hearts advertisement in the *Manchester Weekly Journal*. This action was regarded as so scandalous that the mayor committed her to a lunatic asylum for four weeks.

Despite their shaky beginning, newspaper personals or 'soul mate' ads have become a very popular place to look for a partner. All the daily newspapers run weekly pages of small ads, as do local papers. These are run offline (that is, you can find them on a page in the newspaper) and online, through the newspapers' websites. The pages are divided into female to male, male to female, male to male and female to female ads. It's quite easy to run your eye down the column searching for someone in the right age group or the right part of the country. Advertisers have to lodge their details with the newspaper so you get some security from small ads but you don't get that all-important photograph. However, you can always arrange to e-mail your photos to each other before you meet.

If you read an ad you like the sound of you can phone and listen to a message they've recorded, telling you about them-selves. Alternatively, you can place an advert about yourself for free in the newspaper and record a short audio piece about yourself. You pay premium rates to listen to messages recorded by other people and to hear the replies to your own ad. It can cost up to around £5 for each recorded message and reply. The recorded messages sometimes seem to be padded out with information about the services available but, if you are smart, you can use your telephone buttons to shortcut these service announcements.

Certain newspapers and magazines get a reputation for fun small ads and good places to look for a partner. Ask around to find the right one for you. If you have a particular interest or hobby, then advertising in specialist magazines is a sensible way to contact people with similar tastes. This seems to work well when individuals have a serious hobby, like caving, horse-riding or scuba-diving, which takes up a lot of weekends and holidays.

'I LIKE TO LAUGH IN BED' – WRITING A GREAT 'SOUL MATES' ADVERT

Many romance-seekers go astray when they start writing about themselves and the sort of person they want to meet. Giving the wrong impression in an advertisement can mean the difference between getting hundreds of replies and none at all. You can't expect to tell the whole truth about yourself in 30 words or less so it's better to try to be original and interesting – without bending the truth too far – and so get plenty of replies.

Be Specific and Positive

The idea is to be specific and positive about yourself, and open-minded but clear about the kind of person you want to meet. When you describe yourself, try and be as detailed as possible to make yourself stand out from all the other advertisers. If you read a 'soul mates' column in a news-paper, you will notice that many people describe themselves as 'attractive', but this doesn't say very much about the kind of person they are. Try to draw a mental picture for the reader: 'Alan Sugar with a sense of humour' or 'Anne Robinson lookalike' would be more intriguing. Saying you are interested in films is bland: are you talking about Peruvian arthouse movies or Disney cartoons?

Make sure you include all relevant information about yourself such as age, sex, children, geographical area, marital status. Include your basic preferences but don't be too restrictive. It's surprising how many male advertisers are looking for a blonde Taurean air stewardess aged between 24 and 25. Separated or widowed lonely hearts should beware of trying to find a replica of their lost partner, especially of asking for the same hair colour or height as their former partner.

Many men make the mistake of beginning their advert by describing their ideal woman. For example, 'Leggy, blonde professional is sought by . . .' These ads are unsuccessful because when women readers are running their eyes down the column, they skip over them, thinking they are written by other women. Begin with 'I' messages and don't forget to sell yourself in the first few words of the advert.

Kindness, humour and intelligence are the highest-prized qualities among women. To attract men, emphasise both looks and character along the lines of this highly successful opener: 'Flame-haired bombshell with brains seeks . . .' The author of that ad received 268 replies.

Have a Sense of Humour

When it comes to writing attractive advertisements, people in the romance business agree that a sense of humour is your most important asset, far outweighing good looks or a fat wallet. One highly successful small ad in a magazine brought in 400 replies to the female searcher who wrote 'I like to laugh in bed', while the man who was after 'callipygous, blue-eyed brunettes' got no replies at all. (In case you are wondering, 'callipygous' means 'big-bottomed'!) The most successful adverts are light-hearted and cheeky; the unsuccessful are obscure, pompous or heavy-handed.

Anything that helps to bring you alive on paper is helpful. Beware of common pitfalls, however, such as alliteration. This used to be popular in the days of orange swirly wallpaper but is now seen as dated, along the lines of: 'Cheerful Cantonese chef . . .' or 'Handsome hospital hunk . . .' Some people take it even further with the 'themed ad' but, according to advertising managers, gushing ads like these are a real turn-off these days, unless you are in an ironic or retro frame of mind:

> *Shapely Seafaring Sauceboat, 28, 5'6", seeks handsome trainee Captain who's in the mood for a leisurely sail into the sunset. If you're ready to throw your compass overboard, I'd like to send you off course!*

Advertise in Publications You Read

It may sound obvious but be sure to advertise in the sorts of newspapers and magazines that you normally buy and read yourself. If you advertise in publications you don't like, you will meet people you don't like and don't have anything in common with – no need to say any more!

Be Prepared for Disappointment

You may get no replies at all, or just one or two that are totally unsuitable. In a survey, the majority of the 80 advertisers received 20-30 replies. Four got none at all.

MARYANNE (58) *I met an American professor of English through a magazine advert and we went to shows in London and telephoned each other, nothing romantic. Bill was highly intellectual, short, aggressive and great company. Then he sent me a single ticket to New York. I went. On the drive to his home he said: 'Do you mind if the dogs share our bed?' He added that he was impotent. Well, what could I say?*

A SHORT GUIDE TO EUPHEMISMS AND ABBREVIATIONS

Personals have a language all of their own, and you can be sure that people who use shorthand in their adverts are regulars:

ALA – All letters answered

ALAWP – All letters answered with picture (if you say it, make sure you do it!)

ASL? – Age, sex and location? A question frequently asked on Internet chat sites but to some it feels rude, as if they are trying to buy a prize heifer.

TS – Transsexual

FTM, MTF – Female to male or male to female transsexuals

TV – Transvestite

KNO – Kids no object

NS – Means non-smoker rather than, as some people think, 'no sex'

Discreet, Afternoon meetings, Partnered – married or already living with someone

Strict, Master, Slave, BD, SM – writer has an interest in bondage

Mature, youthful, young at heart – but not in body

SCREENING YOUR REPLIES

Most replies to personal ads these days come in the form of phone messages (charged at premium rates) to your personal box number. Be careful not to erase them accidentally before you've made a note of how to contact the person again (the personal columns are full of ads about lost phone numbers). If you want to stay in touch and avoid the premium rate charges, give out your mobile telephone number, not your landline, for others to contact you on.

Some magazines may also use old-style box numbers for letters sent to you via the magazine. The magazine will collect them up and post them on to you and it might be a while before you receive a package.

Whatever the method of contact, you don't have to reply to any message or letter if you don't want to. Don't let politeness or pity get you into awkward situations.

TWELVE OTHER WAYS TO MEET NEW PEOPLE

For some people, the established dating business isn't the right way to meet new people. Or perhaps you gave it a go but decided it wasn't for you. You can use the confidence-boosting steps in our Positivity Plan (see Chapter 3) to kick-start a braver attitude to meeting new people in any situation (providing you put your personal safety first, of course!).

It doesn't matter how shy you might be, the way to conquer your nerves is to regularly practise being sociable: smiling at people; saying 'hello' to people in the street; asking open questions that show interest and concern without being intrusive or pushy; and generally doing something small each day to boost your friendships and sense of connection with your friends, street, family and community.

When you feel confident about being friendly, think about applying your skills to PPM (Potential Partner Material). Might you get talking to that nice girl on the bus? What might you say to that guy who wraps your bread? So here are 12 other tried and trusted ways to meet new people:

1. Think about **existing groups** you belong to. Could you expand the membership or get to know existing members better? How could you become more proactive in that group? Are there existing groups at your workplace that you've yet to explore? Have you actually confided in your friends that you're looking to meet someone special and asked them to help you?

2. **Social networking.** Socialising in a group can be less threatening than a one-to-one date. Weekend clubs, lunch dates, discos and holidays for singles are a gentler way to get to know new people without committing yourself. There are dozens of social networking organisations with programmes offering different events: country house weekends, flying, ballooning, yoga, skiing, murder-mystery parties, horse-racing and the opera, to name just a few. The organisation Gingerbread organises social events for lone parents.

3. **Address books.** Look back over your address books, even the really old, out-of-date ones, and contact people you used to know and like. If they've moved house, try looking on social networking websites like Facebook to see if you can reconnect with them. It doesn't matter that you've been out of touch for years; a once-close friend will be pleased to hear from you again. Often our social lives get stuck in a rut because we run out of new people to meet inside our friendship group. Reconnecting with old friends expands your circle among the kind of folk whose company you already know you enjoy.

4. **Dining clubs.** The organiser books a restaurant table and invites four or five women and the same number

of men. You aren't paired up in advance but simply introduced to everyone at the beginning of the evening. These dining clubs are a safe place for single women to meet people but some say it's hard to form bonds if you're moving round after each course. However, it's a fun evening with very little risk or awkwardness, and not too expensive. Search for 'dining clubs' online to find one in your city or area.

5. **Voluntary organisations, political parties and charities** are always looking for unpaid help. Working for a cause can be incredibly useful and rewarding and bring a sense of achievement. Pick a cause close to your heart and their offices will be full of like-minded people of all ages and plenty of opportunities for socialising. Or you could join a trade union or professional organisation and get more involved with your work or with wider causes.

6. The **supermarket deli counter** has acquired a sort of mystique as a pick-up joint. How a conversation about the merits of cold meats leads to a date is a mystery but it might be worth a try. You need a pre-prepared line for this endeavour. Perhaps choose an interesting-looking person and say: 'Do you happen to know a good recipe involving celery?'

7. Pick your **adult education class** wisely to meet the right gender. Straight women can sign on for car mechanics and computer courses which tend to attract more men, while romance-seeking gentlemen can tackle cookery and creative writing in order to meet someone nice. Weekend courses and summer schools give even more chance for socialising in a comfortable environment.

8. There are many **sporting singles holidays** on offer. Yoga tends to be mainly female but skiing and diving have a better gender balance. Therapy and creative breaks, according to one large company, attract roughly twice as many women as men. To avoid disappointment, ask about the ratio of women to men before you book as singles holidays generally tend to attract more women than men. Search online for organisations that arrange holidays for people with specific circumstances, such as Young and Widowed, a UK resource, information and holiday website for younger people whose partner has died.

CHRISTINA (32) *I met my husband on a singles holiday. I wasn't expecting it to be a success but by the third evening we were exchanging stories around the pool about how we came to be so desperate as to book a singles holiday. Four of the eight, I think, ended up in bed together and I'm glad to say my relationship continued when we got home.*

9. **Dogs** are the new health club for the noughties. Try flirting in the park while the dogs find their own doggy ways of sizing each other up.

10. Join or start a **residents group** and increase the social contact in your street by throwing a **street party**. Leaflet your road and get a planning group together over a glass of wine or a cup of coffee. Ask for volunteers for each job and plan regular meetings before the event. It's a useful and fun way of being a good neighbour and you'll be amazed how many new faces turn up. The nice thing about a street party is that you can invite anyone you might have spied who looks interesting.

11. Some local listings magazines have a column called 'I Spied You' where you attempt to get in touch with people you admired from afar. As in, 'I spied you at the Tate Modern art gallery. You were wearing a flowery dress and red shoes. Me? Brown hair and green briefcase. I asked you for the time and a jolt of electricity passed through me. If you feel the same way, contact me at box...' Informants say these ads are successful as long as you manage to identify the object of your admiration.

12. **Don't forget to be active.** Do new, active things. Be a good friend: look interested, ask questions and show concern. Never forget that kindness is valued more highly in a partner than looks. Encourage others to make the most of who they are and develop your hobbies into passions.

Okay, so you've winked at each other, you've poked, you've sent a smile, you've sent a letter, you've exchanged chatty e-mails and there's definitely some chemistry and curiosity in evidence on both sides. You get the feeling you're both ready to check out the other in the flesh. The next chapter looks at how to get the most from your first meeting.

Chapter 8

Setting Up the First Meeting

You've used all your proactive skills to get this far so keep thinking positively as you plan to meet up in person. Try to frame the event in your mind as 'expanding my network of friendship' and put aside that naughty little voice that keeps tempting you to think: 'This could be The One.'

A lot of people think they will recognise 'The One' the minute they walk into the room but studies show that only a minority of lovers – between 30 and 40 per cent – were immediately attracted to the person they went on to marry. By getting hung up on 'Do I fancy him or her?' you are closing down your opportunities for proactive dating and will find yourself being constantly disappointed. Nancy, 28, recognised that she had been making this mistake: 'I've been trying to find a clone of my last boyfriend, who I've never really got over,' she said. 'No wonder everyone I meet fails to match up.' If, on the other hand, you go into that coffee shop hoping to make a new friend and expand your social circle, you are likely to feel calmer, more in control and less concerned about the meeting being a flop.

MODERN DATING ETIQUETTE

The longer you've been off the dating scene, the more nervous you're likely to be about meeting someone new. The rules may have changed, or you may feel there are no rules left that you recognise. Even though you may be mature, sexually experienced and perhaps have children, it won't stop you feeling very nervous, especially if your last experience of being in a relationship came to a bruising end.

The first rule is to consult your own feelings and inclinations and do what feels right. Women and men are expected to be more assertive these days and able to stand up for themselves and their own values. This means listening to your own preferences and not being swayed by someone else's agenda. Assertive doesn't mean the same as aggressive. It means knowing your own mind and asserting your own opinions. If you need more help in developing this ability, go back to our Positivity Plan (see Chapter 3), ask a friend for help or maybe speak to a counsellor.

ASKING SOMEONE OUT

These days it's perfectly okay for either a woman or a man to ask the other out. If you've never done this before, you may find this difficult. It takes courage and you have to be prepared for a refusal, something that can come as a real blow. By making the invitation casual, you soften the blow if they say no and make it easier for them to say yes. If you do get a refusal, it might hurt your pride like crazy but try and be a good loser. Wish them well, shake their hand and walk away to lick your wounds somewhere in private, or to talk it through with a close friend.

WHO PAYS THE BILL?

It may surprise you to know that picking up the tab can cause quite a bit of friction on a date. Men, in particular, worry about not getting this right: they don't want to offend by paying, or by *not* paying. Women, also, have differing attitudes; while one will expect to be wined and dined at the man's expense, another sees letting a man pay either as unfair on his wallet or as putting pressure on her to be nicer to him. A cringe-making example of this was a pilot of a small aircraft who complained on his first date: 'I've taken you out for dinner and for a spin in my plane. The least you can do to say thanks is sleep with me!' She didn't give in to this piece of attempted blackmail.

The safest assumption is to split the bill in half. If your date makes a fuss about this, and insists on paying, well, give in graciously and let them. But any kind of black-mailing afterwards is out of line.

TO KISS OR NOT TO KISS

Part of the fun of meeting someone new is expecting the unexpected, especially on a first date. Flirting expert Mary Balfour advises playing it cool but with a little teasing if you want a relationship to grow. 'Instant passion is easy, but the slower and more tantalising the build-up to that first kiss, the more exciting it will be and the more likely it will develop into something special,' she says. She suggests that a slow, lingering brush of lips against cheek at the end of the evening will be enough to intrigue and tantalise.

Her advice is the same when it comes to whether or not to sleep with your date. However tempted you might be in the heat of the moment, taking things too fast is playing Russian roulette with a longer-lasting relationship. (For more on this subject, see Chapter 10.)

ARRANGING A FIRST MEETING

Don't think of using your home landline as this could identify your address and think twice before using your work landline, which will identify your place of work. Personal information should be withheld until you have met and feel you can trust each other. Use your mobile phone or dial 141 (in the UK) before calling so that your caller number will be hidden.

Keep the chat short. Don't be tempted to get into long, flirtatious or sexy conversations at this point as this makes things embarrassing and awkward if you later meet but don't hit it off. Don't forget that your fantasies cannot help but conjure up an image in your mind of someone particularly interesting, and the reality is guaranteed to be not exactly as you have pictured it.

If you make the first call, remember to smile into the receiver and pick a moment when you feel relaxed and calm. Check that it's a good moment to call as you never get the best out of someone when they are about to go into a meeting or cooking the dinner. If it's the wrong moment, you might go away with the strong feeling they're not interested. Think twice before leaving a string of messages as this might be off-putting at the other end. Appearing to be 'too keen' can be a real turn-off, particularly to men.

The proactive dater, as we've already said, sets up several meetings at the same time with the prospect of increasing friendships and practising social skills. So arrange a meeting in a public place like a coffee shop or a bar and keep it short – around an hour could be enough for one drink or a cup of coffee. Make sure it's somewhere you can get to easily, and a good setting for relaxed conversation. It's polite to tell your date that you have another engagement afterwards and what time you'll be leaving.

We say No Dinner on the first date. If there's no spark and a chilly atmosphere between the two of you, that dinner you were looking forward to will turn out to be much more of a chore than a quick drink or a coffee. No cinema and no theatre either, as you'll be sitting next to a stranger and unable to get to know them better.

CARNATION OR ROLLED-UP UMBRELLA?

In order to stay relaxed you will find it easier to meet inside a venue, rather than outside on the street, which is such an exposed place to wait for a stranger, especially in the typical British weather. Don't forget to describe yourself or what you'll be wearing and take a contact phone number.

> DON (25) *I travelled 120 miles on the train and waited in the International Hotel Bar for two hours. My date, meanwhile, was sitting in the International Youth Hostel Bar about 100 yards up the road. Neither of us had the other's telephone number. We never did meet up – it just wasn't meant to be, was it?*

MAKING A GOOD IMPRESSION

The personality qualities prized by romance-seekers of both sex are confidence, optimism, independence, curiosity, kindness, intelligence and a sense of humour. According to flirting expert Mary Balfour, men who chose to have second dates with her clients used words to describe them such as optimistic, relaxed, confident, direct, kind, humorous, fun, approachable and friendly.

So how does this impact on you as you prepare for your first date? If you feel your best qualities don't always come across because you are anxious or shy – and we've all been there – then spend some time working with our Positivity Plan in order to tame your anxieties before you start your search (see Chapter 3).

LOOKING YOUR BEST

Psychological studies of Western men reveal what they find attractive in women: long hair, smooth skin, regular features, big 'Bambi' eyes, small waist and a generous mouth. However, when it comes to finding a mate with whom to have children, men consistently prefer two qualities – kindness and intelligence – and are prepared to trade off looks in order to capture a mate with these qualities. This may be because they feel that less beautiful women are less likely to be attractive to other men and unfaithful to them.

Women are not so driven by good looks as men but they do seem to be interested in the status and earning power of a male partner. Studies show that men prefer to marry women of slightly lower social status than themselves. The evolutionary explanation for this difference is that women seek a mate who will, above all, provide for them and their children. Men may seek lower-status women because they unconsciously believe they can more easily keep control of them. Falling in love, then, say the scientists, is basically a process where both sides feel they're getting a good enough deal.

Mary Balfour's advice about looks is: if you're looking for love, don't be too proud to make the most of your appearance. Get advice from a trusted friend in order to feel that you are presenting yourself in the best possible way. **Ask yourself: does the way I look and dress portray my character to the best advantage?** If not, consider spending some time and, inevitably, money on changing things.

DRESSING FOR COMFORT OR STYLE?

It may be tempting to dress to impress. However, first-date feedback shows that, as a general rule, you will feel more relaxed if you dress comfortably in a familiar outfit rather than trying too hard and ending up feeling stiffly overdressed.

> SIMONE (28) *I made the mistake of wearing a new wrapover black and white dress and the tie kept loosening at the front, à la Judy Finnegan at the awards ceremony. I spent the date trying to stop the dress falling open and revealing my bra or pants, or both!*

You are who you are. This book's philosophy is that you enjoy and relish yourself just as you are rather than listening to voices in the media lecturing you to be thinner, younger, taller, smoother, trendier; to wear brighter colours, neutral colours, pink spots, balloon skirts, gladiator boots, fur capes . . . or whatever! Just forget all those pressurising voices for a moment and concentrate on what *you* like and what *you* feel good in. And then, when you feel daring, consult a trusted friend about how you come across to other people.

Do this at a time when you feel relaxed and receptive to the opinions of others. Rather than asking for 'criticism' of your appearance, put a different spin on it: what colours suit you? What styles look good on you? And which outfit does your friend like best? However, in the interests of research, you might be surprised to read the list overleaf, compiled by Mary Balfour, of some of the first-date feedback mentioned by men who joined her agencies:

Men's Top Dating Turn-offs

1. Broody women-in-a-hurry – come across as desperate and on the hunt for a sperm donor.
2. Smoking – those who admit to smoking find it harder to get dates.
3. Dates who avoid direct eye contact.
4. 'Granny clothes' – lots of gold jewellery, pearls (seen as 'mumsy'), dangly earrings, too much make-up, scarves or baggy clothes.
5. Too much blue, green or pearly eye shadow.
6. Interrupting him.
7. Annoying laughs or loud sniffs.
8. Negative body language such as stooping or folded arms, and bad posture generally.
9. Closely cropped hair – however fashionable and gamine, this is often cited by men as a turn-off and a denial of femininity.
10. Roots that need retouching.
11. Glasses – seen on the first date by some as a barrier to communication. Later in a relationship, though, they don't seem to matter. Mary advises: 'Use them as a flirting prop. You could whip them off from time to time to reveal your eyes directly.'
12. Overdressing – 'can make women look needy'.

Women's Top Dating Turn-offs

After taking a straw poll among the women who were interviewed for this book, top female turn-offs include the following:

1. Being too earnest or humourless – 'Talked about his job for an hour… and his job was spot welding.'
2. Wearing strange, archaic clothes chosen by his mum – 'canary yellow shirt with a blue jacket'.

3. Smoking – even smokers don't want to go out with smokers.
4. Talking continually about himself – 'Didn't seem at all interested in my life.'
5. Poor personal profile – 'His profile was short, scrappy and badly written: bad spelling and even worse grammar.'
6. Caginess – 'He hasn't uploaded a picture to his Internet profile but won't chat unless he gets one from me first.'
7. Being too keen – 'He wanted to come round this afternoon and help me decorate my house, even though we'd never met or spoken before.'
8. Being too sexual – 'As I was trying to leave, he asked if I wanted to go around to his flat for sex.'

These lists back up psychologists' research about some of the differences between women and men when it comes to finding a partner. Men tend to be visually driven, physically turned on and want immediate rewards – yes, that means sex. Women tend to be less concerned about looks and more interested in personality and communication abilities.

SUCCESSFUL SMALL TALK

Some people just hate small talk. They don't know how to do it and they think it's a waste of time. They'd rather inform the other person about something they find fascinating, be it football or the Middle East. However, on a first date, think small talk before big talk. You're trying to find out about the other person and to draw out the best in them and yourself. In order to do that, you need to be sensitive to the pace of their self-disclosure. In other words, small talk is the talk that oils the conversation and helps to establish a genuine bond. Big talk can turn into a one-sided lecture. Small talk can help both parties relax as well as bringing a sense of lightness, balance and give-and-take to the exchange. It doesn't have to be boring and can lead, naturally, to more interesting topics of chat.

BUT HELP! I'M SHY AND TONGUE-TIED

You are not alone. And take heart in the fact that you're meeting someone who's likely to be as jittery as you are. In fact, admitting 'I feel nervous' is one of the best ice-breakers around.

Fortunately, the art of conversation is on the side of the shy and tongue-tied. The good conversationalist will listen more than they talk, will take pleasure in deepening the topic with a string of appropriate questions and will show that they've heard the answers. So have a think beforehand about what you're likely to have in common. If you can pick out a shared interest, such as hill-walking or cinema, you have a ready-made topic of conversation that should see you through the hour in style. Make a mental note of hot topics in the newspapers and television news in the days leading up to your date to provide yourself with material for some lively conversation.

One effective technique for keeping the conversation moving is to ask your companion open questions such as: 'Tell me more about that'; 'What will you do?'; 'How did you feel about that?' When the conversation turns to you, being upbeat comes over as much more attractive than being over-modest or grumbling about your life. Instead of saying, 'My life is a bit boring. I've two kids and a part-time job in the local hardware store,' try presenting yourself in a more positive light: 'My kids are great fun, I love being with them and though it's not my ideal job, I always end up having a laugh.'

To support yourself further, pay attention to your posture. Straighten your spine if you feel stressed. This allows you to breathe deeply and has a calming effect. You will naturally feel more confident and more attractive. When we are nervous, we tend to gabble and not listen properly. Psychological studies show that men are the worst offenders: they take up more airtime than women and have absolutely no idea they're doing it. If you eavesdrop on a conversation going on over your shoulder, you might notice this phenomenon: in a mixed group, women tend to be better listeners than men because they are socialised to put other people's needs first.

But hey, it's the 21st century and you don't have to be a martyr about this. Perhaps you could switch off a conversation-hogger by simply asking: 'So, what would you like to know about me?' However, if your PPM is gabbling because he or she is nervous, you could try to rescue the situation by showing some compassion and acknowledging the awkwardness of the situation. For example, you could smile and say something encouraging like: 'I'm really interested in what you're saying.' By drawing attention to how the two of you are communicating at that very moment, you might shift the chat into a more balanced place and actually start finding the talk a lot more interesting.

WHAT NOT TO TALK ABOUT

Women are just as bad as men at breaking the golden rule of first dates. This should be etched on all our foreheads: never talk about why your last relationship ended. It's not surprising that this topic should be uppermost in our thoughts much of the time. We may be feeling raw or vulnerable following a separation or divorce; perhaps missing our children and having to share them with an ex-partner; or feeling tortured by grief or anger over the end of a long relationship. But please believe me when I say that it would be too much, too soon to get into a deep conversation about loss, anger and grief. However sympathetic the listener may be, experience shows that they may feel overwhelmed by your story when they reflect on it after the date. This may lead them to cancelling any future meetings.

If you feel you may have difficulty *not* talking about your ex-partner, discuss it with a friend beforehand. Perhaps you can agree on a gracious phrase if the subject comes up, along the lines of: 'Oh, that's too long a story to get into now.' Similarly, if your date starts talking about a very difficult subject – illness, custody battles, anger or death – think how you will handle that. You may feel a great deal of compassion for them but is it what you need on a first date? After the event, they may also feel foolish and that they've 'given too much away', and their embarrassment can easily be a deal-breaker which stops them contacting you again.

INTERESTED? NOT INTERESTED? NOT SURE?

Before the date, it's a good idea to think about how to signal your intentions at the end of the meeting. You want to avoid causing embarrassment or ending things on a bad note. It's easy to get caught out and wrong-footed, especially if your date is a regular on the dating scene and goes out on dozens of dates with different people. These people can be spotted because they are usually very direct. Within minutes of meeting you they may say, 'You're not my type really,' or, 'I'm very attracted to you and want to see you again tomorrow.'

If you're not expecting this direct, upfront approach, it can come as a shock to be judged so quickly and casually and, sometimes, brutally. But try not to take it personally – this directness is a feature of the Internet dating scene and is not a putdown of you or how loveable you are. In fact, for many British people who have been brought up with a 'stiff upper lip', it can even seem quite refreshing to be on the receiving end of the direct approach.

Using your proactive style, try and get in touch with how *you* feel about him or her rather than being railroaded by the other person's opinions. You might think someone who can make brutal and swift judgements isn't worth a second date anyway! You'll also meet plenty of sensitive people who don't treat their date in such a businesslike manner, or who may be on their first date for many years and not have a clue how to handle it.

Experienced dater Jasmine, who manages to combine directness with sensitivity to people's feelings, recommends the following:

If you're not interested in meeting again say: 'Thank you so much for meeting me and I've enjoyed this drink but I don't think we're compatible, do you?' If you definitely feel you want to meet again say something like: 'It feels to me like we might have a lot in common and shall we take it from here?' When you're not sure whether or not to go for a second date, say: 'Shall we go away and think about it?'

Jasmine's approach has the advantage of suggesting it's a *joint* decision whether or not to meet again. Having been on something like 60 dates, she feels she knows her own mind quite quickly but her dates may not be as clear as she is. Sometimes, after thinking about it overnight, she changes her mind and decides she would like to meet a man for a second date. However, there is one drawback to the 'think it over' gambit: if you are not interested in a second meeting, you may feel obliged to ring and say so. Netiquette – the standards of conduct expected on the Internet – doesn't require these high standards of politeness. A simple e-mail saying, 'Thanks but I don't think we have enough in common,' is a polite but firm way to terminate contact with someone.

This is the strategy adopted by Nicola who, like a lot of 30-somethings, finds her social circle is full of close friends who see a lot of each other but this doesn't give her the opportunity to meet new and interesting men. Nicola runs all her dating through the Internet and has made a lot of new friends that way:

> NICOLA (34) *I meet people in the public bar of my local pub. I have a formula: a glass of wine, a nice chat and then, after about an hour, my female flatmate appears at our table and we say goodbye, thanks for meeting and let's e-mail in a couple of days. That gives us both a breathing space without seeming rude.*

On the other hand, if you really like someone, don't let the evening end without suggesting another meeting. It's all too easy to end a first date with no firm plans and then, because each side is afraid of rejection, neither wants to be the first to phone the other to suggest another date. At the end of a good evening, you could say: 'I've enjoyed meeting you and it would be nice to see you again. Can I give you a ring in the next few days?' This is a clear statement without trying to pressurise your date into committing themselves.

DEALING WITH DIFFICULT SITUATIONS

The vast majority of people you will meet in your search for love will be upright and genuine. But there's no point in denying that the dating game does attract a few sad, inadequate or dodgy people of both sexes. When speaking on the phone or in person, you need to stow away whatever codes of politeness you were raised with and replace them with an unswerving instinct for your own safety and wellbeing.

'Thanks for a nice evening but I don't want to meet up again' is a more straightforward and assertive way of behaving than ending an evening you have no intention of repeating with: 'Well, er, it might be nice to meet up again, sometime, maybe?' If you say the latter, don't be surprised if you get bombarded with messages until you make it clear that you've decided not to see them again.

If you do enough dating, one or two people will press your buttons, especially if you can't say no and give out a vague and inconsistent message about possible future meetings. They might get upset and plead for another date or want to come around to your house. They may offer to take you home and make sexual overtures. They may turn offensive if they don't get what they want. They may phone you 20 times a day. How are you going to handle these difficult situations and calm things down?

Practise saying 'No' clearly but with some sensitivity. Try out some assertive phrases. Roll them around on your tongue and get used to giving a straight message – this can be particularly difficult for older daters with strong ideas of what is polite and impolite. It can be useful if you have a close friend who is prepared to help you practise.

The following is an extreme example of things going wrong but it shows that the worst could happen if you don't follow your instincts. I know – because it was me it happened to.

BARBARA (40) *We met in a wine bar in the King's Road. My date was standing by the bar dressed in an Afghan coat and looked just like Big Daddy, the wrestler – bearded, about 6 foot 4 inches and heavily built.*

Right from the start his conversation made me uncomfortable and I wished I'd left straightaway. At one point he asked if I would like to go to his place for an 'orgy' but I laughed it off. Searching for a safe topic of conversation, I asked about his hobbies and he said 'shooting', reached into a plastic bag under the table and brought out an air pistol which he waved around under the table, out of other people's view.

I was really scared but didn't want to show it. Neither did I want to inflame the situation. I felt frozen, not sure what to do for the best – call for help or run out of the wine bar. I got up quickly, made a hasty and over-polite goodbye and left. Once I was out of sight, I ran up the road to a department store and hid behind some rolls of fabric in the haberdashery department. I really felt he might follow me.

He did. Looking out of the store's window into the street, there was my date standing, looking around. After 15 minutes of searching for me he disappeared into the underground station. When I got home, there was a string of messages waiting from him. I told my flatmate, Simon, and got him to phone back saying I didn't want to see him again.

The agency that put us together promised to blacklist him and I also phoned the police as I feared he might start stalking me. If I'd trusted my initial instincts that this man sounded creepy over the phone, and been clearer about my boundaries, all that followed would have been avoided.

COPING WITH REJECTION

Rejection hurts, no matter how sensitively it is delivered. Sooner or later, you are likely to experience rejection by one or more of your dates. Whether it's delivered in person, on the phone or by e-mail or text, rejection is difficult to deal with. Even if the rejection comes as a bit of a relief, it may still be a shock.

Jasmine, a veteran romancer, says that experienced daters become very direct and start to make instant judgements:

> *I had barely finished my coffee when one guy said: 'Well, I don't think we're compatible and I've got someone else to see.' And then he left, slapping down a pound coin on the table for his drink. The whole thing shocked me. Another time, there was quite a build-up on the phone with the owner of a rich, beautiful voice. He was flattering and sexy and keen to meet me. I hesitated because it meant driving 50 miles each way but he sounded so lovely. After a few weeks we did meet in person and were having lunch in a country pub when he suddenly announced: 'I'm actually living with someone but thought I might prefer you. But now I've met you, I think I'm doing the right thing staying with her.'*

If you're not careful, these weird outbursts of honesty can damage your self-esteem and cause you to doubt your own judgement. But Jasmine, a proactive dater, always makes sure she has other interesting profiles and romantic leads on the backburner so she can retain the hope and optimism for her love quest.

There is a lot to be said for a direct approach that doesn't keep someone hanging around, fruitlessly yearning and hoping for things to develop. But, if you've been out of the romance scene for some years, you will be surprised by the directness that some daters show, particularly the cyber-lovers. With the spread of the Internet dating business, it feels like some see a partner as a commodity to be traded, or love as a purchase to be made in a supermarket.

On the other hand, all experienced daters will have had those times when the date goes well and ends with eager promises to call each other very soon for a second meeting. When you get home, *you* might be the one with second thoughts and, having slept on it, decide you don't want to repeat the outing. Or the same could have happened at the other end.

Try to be philosophical and not see this as a personal rejection of you as a human being. Notch it up to the swings and roundabouts of life until it becomes a funny story for the pub. All our lives are complex and you don't know what is going on in the life of your date, what pressures and responsibilities they are juggling, so try and stay compassionate if they seem to turn you down in a thoughtless way. Keep thinking the best of them or give them some gentle feedback about their manner, which may help their next date.

Being rejected by someone is bad enough, but having to be the one doing the rejecting is also difficult for most of us. It can be tempting to just 'accidentally lose' their telephone number and avoid the ending altogether. However, making a clean ending is all part of taking responsibility for your future happiness, and frankness is an important, adult life skill we all need to learn. If you are the one who is doing the rejecting, try and find a constructive but clear way to give the news. For example: 'I've loved hearing about your passion for water-skiing but I'm not sure we have enough shared interests, are you?' If you discuss your doubts with the other person, their responses might change your mind – or not.

On the other hand, daters often come back to someone they've rejected earlier, once they've built up some courtship savvy and have a better sense of the sort of partner they are looking for. This is what Ali learned in the course of many dates over six months. Once he had begun to relax a bit and enjoyed making new friends in the gay community, he began to understand the rules of the game and stopped being so picky about the brains, looks and status of the men he was meeting. He reconnected with Simon, someone he had dated at the beginning and turned down as not being tall enough! This time around, they clicked and started a long-term relationship.

TIPS FOR COPING WITH REJECTION

➤ Proactive dating, where you keep up a friendly but calm interest in several people at the same time, helps to keep your confidence steady in the early stages of dating and softens the blow of rejection.

➤ If you get rejected on a first meeting, don't take it personally. Wish them well and go on to the next lead. At the same time, perhaps have a frank chat with a close friend to find out if you have an off-putting personal habit – like sniffing or humming – that you could easily get rid of.

➤ If someone you have been seeing for a while rejects you in a callous way, let them know how you feel and then move on.

➤ Timing is everything. Someone who doesn't click with you at the moment might be in a different place in six months' time.

TIPS FOR REJECTING SENSITIVELY

➤ Be kind, truthful and straightforward and treat others respectfully so they can move on feeling okay about themselves.

➤ Trust your instincts and don't let compassion or pity change your mind. But remember that in a few months' time, you might feel differently about someone who's a 'no' at this point.

➤ Don't reject a second date by text message. E-mail is acceptable netiquette after a first date but the telephone is better if you've been seeing them for a while.

➤ Don't leave someone hanging on or ignore their phone calls or e-mails just because you're too cowardly to turn them down. And don't stand someone up or just not turn up at all, unless you want the same things to happen to you.

MARTHA (43) *Coming out of a 12-year relationship and trying to find somebody, I wanted to fill the gap straight-away. On a local newspaper website I met an airline pilot – professional, articulate and funny. We went out for three months. One day he came into the room dressed in S&M gear. I thought, 'No, that's not my scene,' and it ended there and then.*

DO'S AND DON'TS FOR A SUCCESSFUL AND SAFE FIRST DATE

➤ DO check your phone manner and answerphone message to sound warm and welcoming.

➤ DO arrange a time when you feel relaxed. Meeting after a hard day's slog may not be a good idea.

➤ DO make your first meeting a low-key affair, like a cup of coffee in a public place. It should last no more than an hour or so.

➤ DO remember it's just a coffee; they're not necessarily 'The One'.

➤ DO prearrange how you will recognise each other and meet inside a suitable venue.

➤ DO wear something you feel comfortable in.

➤ DO tell someone beforehand where you are going and with whom and prioritise your personal safety.

➤ DO say you feel nervous – always a good ice-breaker.

➤ DO have a phrase ready if you do or don't want to see the person again, or if you're not sure.

➤ DO suggest another meeting if you really like them.

➤ DO offer to pay your share of the bill.

➤ DON'T hide behind a pillar and then stand him or her up – they might do the same to you.

➤ DON'T expect too much. Proactive dating means trying to expand your circle of friends wherever possible.

➤ DON'T go to a cinema or theatre as you won't have time to talk.

➤ DON'T talk about why your last relationship broke up or your bitter custody battle for the children.

➤ DON'T give out your home or work landline number or address until you're sure you can trust them. Use a mobile instead.

➤ DON'T travel in another person's car or go to their home until you know them a lot better.

TAKE A DEEP BREATH...

When you have been out of the dating scene for some time the first date can be a nerve-wracking experience. Remember that the person you are meeting is a human being with their own insecurities and fears, so aim to make the event playful and fun. Approach your date as if you are going out to meet a friend and you will have a fun time. You will want to be as relaxed as possible so enlist a close friend to help you achieve the feel and look you want. Take a good look at yourself; try to be kind by focusing on your best attributes, then highlight them. For example, if you are proud of your long legs don't cover them with a full-length dress. A flirty skirt that finishes at the knee would be perfect!

Think about how you want the date to go, and perhaps write this in your journal. If you are clear about how you want to be, you are much more likely to achieve it. Concentrate on how you want to feel before, during and after the date. Plan enough time so that you can enjoy yourself as you get ready and avoid getting flustered. We are much more attractive when we are relaxed and having fun. Keep up the Positivity Plan strategies outlined in Chapter 3 and work on the mind chatter, letting go of the negative. Keep it all playful. You can never have too much fun!

Go and dazzle.

Chapter 9

Developing the Relationship

The first six months of a new relationship are a journey of discovery about each other. As you move from the second to the third date and beyond, enjoy the feeling of intoxication that comes with a new love, but try not to let it overwhelm your every waking moment – yes, this is easy to say and hard to do! A few daters forget the rules about taking it slowly and find themselves talking all night long, unable to break away from each other's company, and seeing a romantic dawn coming up together. At these moments, there is a sense of chemistry and a sexual frisson with your new love that's hard to resist.

The drawback to this heady, full-on passion in the early days is burn-out and the fear associated with losing one's sense of self. Burn-out feels like 'too much, too soon'. It is a feeling of fear activated by too much disclosure or intimacy too soon in the relationship. You might feel it, for example, after an intense, heady date in which you've laid your vulnerability on the table or sat and listened to the other person's feelings.

Denzil's problem with finding love was repeatedly losing his sense of independence when in a relationship. He explained that he felt drawn into his ex-wife's world of passionate, addiction-fuelled dramas and crises and became hooked on trying to rescue her and provide for her needs. In doing so, though, he lost all sense of himself and of having a choice about whether or not he wanted to be in the relationship. He had quickly become a man who was always reacting to his ex's latest drama. Denzil recognised his problem and worked on his patterns with a counsellor.

The way to avoid falling into familiar but unhelpful patterns is to keep checking yourself and listening to both your head and your heart. You might recall that in Chapter 2 we looked at unconscious reasons why people pair up in order to get the other person to enact the quality they fear in themselves. For example, if you'll be the strict one, I'll be the nice one.

It might help to consider whether your new partner is taking on a role or a task that you personally dislike doing, such as being strict with children, paying bills on time, tidying the home or organising your social life. Obviously, couples have *complementary* interests and skills – this is what brings two people together – but if you feel yourself slipping back into the same unhelpful, rigid patterns or roles that you had with your ex, it might be useful to have some counselling sessions to explore this.

HOW TO SPOT A LIMITING RELATIONSHIP

Milly, who was 34 going on 17, noticed that she always chose partners who were quite a bit older and better off than herself. The unspoken bargain seemed to be that she didn't mind being the lovely eye-candy in the passenger seat as long as he didn't mind paying for the meals and holidays. Lars, her latest boyfriend, who was 52 going on 17, felt she kept him young and was happy to have such a sweet and girlish companion.

Two years or so into her relationships, however, Milly would start to find them limiting and would try and change them. She noticed a pattern: when she started wanting to take control of the bills or decide on a colour scheme for the flat, her partners held on to the purse strings, and didn't want to give up control. Like Milly, Lars found it difficult to be close, intimate and equal. He resented her attempts to change the relationship and told her it was over.

Milly and Lars is a simple example of a couple fit that works well in the beginning but quickly outgrows itself. The unspoken agreement they had made at the start wasn't flexible enough to develop into something that would enable them both to grow as separate people. On the other hand, the opposite could have happened and Lars could have decided to take a chance, step outside his comfort zone and give more power to his girlfriend. So a 'limiting' relationship (or you could call it a 'dysfunctional couple fit') contains the seeds for the development of both individuals, if they have the courage to take a chance.

Think carefully if you notice any of the following patterns developing in your relationship:

He/she reminds you of previous partners. So don't forget why *those* relationships failed.

He/she looks exactly like a previous partner. Are you trying to rewrite a happy ending of your bad relationship?

She/he says they need you desperately. Have you played the rescuer role before?

She/he loves or is married to someone else. Are you avoiding closeness by picking someone unobtainable?

You feel you could help them to have a happier life. Here comes that rescuer again.

You feel really safe around them, as if you're with a mother or father figure. But when you want to grow up, will he or she let you?

He's/she's nasty to you but it's because they had a rotten childhood. It's the rescuer again – you can't change other people, only they can do that.

The two of you never stop arguing. Which of you is afraid of intimacy?

He/she puts you on a pedestal and takes away the ladder. But how long before the fantasy evaporates and you stop being a saint?

He/she is over 35 and has never been in a long-term relationship. So why start now? It looks like they might be scared of closeness.

He/she treats you very well, cares about you and is super-supportive. If you find it difficult to be treated so well, look at why that might be: are you afraid of falling in love and getting hurt or does your low self-confidence say you don't deserve such good treatment?

He/she is physically, financially or emotionally abusive. Has this happened to you before? Put your safety first and get support or counselling as a matter of urgency. See the back of this book for some numbers to call.

Sometimes, when you become aware of a limiting 'fit' to your relationship and are both prepared to work on it, the results can be rewarding for both people in terms of personal growth. But this shouldn't be at the expense of your safety or happiness.

PLANNING FOR THE FUTURE

At Relate we're often surprised by the important topics that couples *don't* talk about or avoid talking about, either consciously or unconsciously. These might include traumatic events that one of the couple or both experienced in childhood, such as bereavement or abuse. The survivor might have mentioned it once in passing but never paused to consider whether this might be still affecting them in some way.

Sometimes a new couple tries to have a conversation about feelings but it goes wrong. Women are usually credited with wanting to talk about feelings all the time, while men feel comfortable with a different style of conversation that is directed towards problem-solving. It's not that men are bad listeners but they tend to view talking about problems as unhelpfully repetitive or navel-gazing. The partner who wants to talk about emotional difficulties – let's say it's the woman – tends to give up trying to communicate with the other because they cannot see how to get satisfaction from the conversation. They don't feel listened to. The other half, meanwhile, feels annoyed or niggled with himself because he can't solve the problem from his partner's past except to tell her: 'It's a shame what happened to you, but stop dwelling on it.'

If you're not careful, this mismatch in conversation – a common difference between women and men – turns into a habit of non-communication that leads to a break-up. Women often say that when they want to offload their feelings they will go to female friends rather than to a partner, while men complain that their wives are always going over the same old ground or want to plan for the future all the time.

In a new relationship, when you're dying to find out all about the other person, you have a great opportunity to develop good communication skills. A simple technique for better communication is to put aside a short time once a week to talk and listen to each other without interruption. You'll need to agree a day and a precise time when you're both going to be able to give this task your full attention, and a regular slot will help make it happen. Agree in advance how much time each person will get – 10 or 15 minutes each is perfect – and set a clock or a timer to let you know when to switch over.

Toss a coin to decide who goes first. The next 10 or 15 minutes is their time to talk about something important to them. The listening partner should not interrupt and must promise to give their full, encouraging attention, really trying to hear what the partner is saying – and no eye-rolling or sighing if the other says something they don't like. The only rule is not to talk about the relationship or blame the other person, but to stick to 'I messages' ('I feel . . . I think . . . I wonder if . . . I like it when . . .') and topics that are close to your heart: planning for the future, thinking about the past or talking about how you're feeling right now.

It doesn't have to be about problems. It could be about successes and complimentary things too, such as: 'Thanks so much for cleaning the kitchen, it looks great.' After 10 or 15 minutes, swap places and let the other talk. At the end, draw a line under the conversation and don't let the discussion limp on or start an argument about what the other person said.

If you do this regularly, it will become easier with practice and you'll feel more bonded with your partner. By investing a small amount of time in actively listening to your partner, you won't suffer like the couple who fell in love during a whirlwind courtship and found themselves in counselling six weeks before their wedding day. They were asked to write separate answers to some questions, including: 'What are your thoughts about having children?'

The female client told the counsellor: 'I want to start our first baby right away.' The man answered: 'I don't want to have children.' In a state of shock, the couple made the decision in the counselling session to postpone their wedding but later managed to find a way to go forward together.

ACTIVE LISTENING EXERCISE

The exercise outlined above is one of the most powerful promoters of a good marriage or partnership. When used regularly, it improves teamwork and the sense that both people are contributing to the success of the relationship. The trick is to make a regular commitment to carrying out this exercise at a time that suits you both. Fill in the following, photocopy it and stick it on the fridge to remind you of your goals:

Where will we hold our regular talking and listening sessions (kitchen, sitting room, garden, etc.)?
....

How many times per week will we hold our sessions (once, twice or three times) and which days of the week?
....

How long will we each speak for (5 minutes, 10 minutes, 15 minutes)?
....

How will we ensure we're not disturbed?
....

How will we ensure we don't get into blaming or a row?
....

What might we discuss? (Put your initials next to any topics that appeal to you or write down some new ones of your own.)

Work
My work
Your work
Future work plans
Something else to do with work
....

Children
Your children
My children
Our children
Pocket money
Discipline
Teenagers
School
Play
Homework
Something else to do with children
....

Money
My money
Your money
Our money
What to spend it on
Not enough?
Savings
Something else to do with money
....

Friends/Family
My family
Your family
Socialising
My friends
Your friends
Our friends
How I'd like our social life to be
Something else to do with friends/family

....

Interests and hobbies
My hobbies
Your hobbies
Our hobbies
What could we do together?
Something else to do with hobbies

....

Feelings
How I felt before
How I feel now
How I want to feel
What I love about you
What I'd like to be different in our relationship
Something else to do with feelings

....

Sex
How I show I love you
How you show you love me
What I'd like for our sexual relationship
Something else to do with sex

....

Home
What I love about it
What I'd like to be different
Sharing the chores
Something else to do with home

....

What I want most from life
My hopes for the future
Your hopes for the future
Our hopes for the future
How can we grow as people?
My fears
Something else to do with the future

....

DEVELOPING THE RELATIONSHIP IF YOU HAVE CHILDREN

Considering two people's emotions in a new relationship is hard enough, but when children are involved it makes things even more complex. Of course, you need to be aware of the needs of your children, but you also have the right to an adult relationship so it's a constant balancing act of needs. Twenty-five per cent of children will experience their parents' separation or divorce before the age of 16, so it's common for children to have to come to terms with Mum or Dad wanting to meet another partner – and deep down they will want to see you happy.

How can you make it easier on the children when you want to introduce a new person into the family? It depends on the age of your children and how you parted from your ex. Children of single parents can find it hard when they are asked to share your love, especially if they've had you to themselves for all or much of their lives. For other children, separation from a dad or mum might be recent and raw, which will bring up different challenges.

If you are a parent who wants to take a chance on love again, it might be a good idea to start dating quietly, without mentioning it to your children, just in case things go wrong or it makes them feel insecure. In fact, it's a good idea to keep the whole thing extremely low-key until you've got a handle on dating again and feel like you're more or less in control of the situation.

This might mean that you cannot sleep with a new partner in your own home in case the children disturb you and are shocked. This would depend on the age of your children and whether they are in the habit of wandering into your bedroom in the middle of the night. If your new partner is committed to a lasting relationship, he or she will respect your reasons for taking the relationship's early stages slowly and carefully for the sake of the children.

If all goes well, at some point you'll want to introduce him or her to your kids. Don't rush into this. Timing is important. If you have recently separated, give your children plenty of time to get used to a new home and new arrangements for custody – it might be two homes they are getting used to. When a couple separates, there are so many changes they are asked to cope with – different homes, different schools, different friendships – and they will need plenty of time to accept that the relationship is over and the split is permanent.

Relationship expert and author of the Relate guide, *Help Your Children Cope with Your Divorce*, Paula Hall, advises: 'Take it slowly. New love has a tendency to blind us to other people's feelings and become overly anxious, but the reality is that if you're really in love you'll easily cope with taking the time that children need to adjust to the ending of your last relationship and the beginning of a new one.'

Children often harbour hopes and fantasies that their parents will get back together again. Separation is likely to make them regress to an earlier stage of development. Depending on their age, they may become clingy, demanding, needy, quiet and 'good', or angry and 'naughty'. By becoming 'younger' they may hope to get things back as they once were, when they were little kids. They experience loss and grief over the split, just like the parents, so this changed behaviour is their way of living the grief stages outlined in Chapter 1 (see page 21).

When children move between homes, they are constantly reminded that the family is no longer together. Children may experience separation anxiety from one or both parents, or they may worry about the wellbeing of the parent they are leaving behind. As one child put it: 'Wherever I am, I'm always missing one or other of you.' If there is goodwill between you and your ex to put the needs of your children first, try to work together to ensure they have familiar belongings and favourite toys with them at each location.

Paula Hall suggests that children can be afraid a new partner will get in the way of their relationship with the other parent. They may become angry and resentful and try to get you onside by making comparisons between the two. Alternatively, they may wish to spend more time with a parent who is on their own, without a partner. The child tries to compensate by caring or providing companionship for a lonely parent. There is so much room for confusion as young people try to juggle their divided loyalties for each parent and for the new partner.

Try and calm the swirling emotions by speaking respectfully in front of the children about your ex and his/her new partner and family. They will learn by the way you model the conversations about family members, so if you can be disciplined and keep back any negative feelings in front of them, you will help children to feel calmer about the situation. Paula adds: 'All of these confused feelings about separation are very natural and will pass in time if they are handled sensitively. Children just need to feel they can share their fears and anxieties, and that they are supported in adjusting to change.'

You can help children by trying to maintain visits with old friends and family members. You might need to take the initiative with this as, when parents split, children can lose touch with some members of your ex's family who felt the need to 'take sides'. It's difficult to explain to young children, for instance, why they cannot see their cousins at the moment. One way of handling it is to ask relatives to remain neutral and friendly, for the sake of all the children. However, this isn't always possible as feelings can run high, especially in cases where one partner has had an affair or there has been abusive behaviour in the relationship. You may need to accept that a rift has happened and live with it for now. Is there a family member who has a reputation for being a 'healer' who could be asked to make a low-key attempt to mend the rift?

Marly found it difficult to deal with her husband's large family when they first got together. Dan had four children by two women, and much of his free time was spent trying to be a good dad to each of them. This didn't leave a lot of time for the new relationship. Trying not to rock the boat with Dan, Marly took out some of her frustrations on Jenna, Dan's first ex-wife, whom she felt was too dependent on them. This led to bad feeling but, fortunately, Marly realised that she needed to calm herself down before she alienated Jenna's children with her complaining. Marly developed her own interests and gradually began to feel more comfortable about her place in this new family jigsaw.

If you can, try and keep the new partner and the relationship break-up as separate events that are not linked with each other. The children may not want to accept your new partner if they think he or she is responsible for the split or trying to replace your ex-partner. Leaving around 12 months between the split and forging a new partnership seems to be a gap that many families have found useful.

HOW TO HANDLE THE FIRST MEETING

Paula Hall suggests preparing for the first meeting by casually mentioning that you've met someone and letting the children know when you're going out to meet them. Their curiosity will build and they will soon start asking questions, but don't be tempted to bring home your new partner without warning.

Paula says: "'What's he/she like? Where do they live? Do they have children? Are you going to get married?' Your children are likely to get to the nitty-gritty much earlier than you think. The deeper question underpinning all these is: "How much impact is this person going to have on my life?"'

Try to be as frank as you can but don't push things. If young children seem to be putting off a meeting, you may need to encourage them by organising an outing such as a trip to the zoo or to a playground. It's better to have the meeting away from the family home, which may be laden with confused feelings for the children, but not all meetings have to be treats as this can lead young people to have unrealistic expectations.

WHEN THERE'S DOMESTIC VIOLENCE OR ABUSE

Sometimes ex-partners react badly to a new man-friend or woman-friend coming on the scene. This could happen out of the blue or it could be a continuance of abuse or violence that happened while you were still with your ex. Domestic violence or abuse covers a wide spectrum of behaviour, not just physical violence like hitting or pushing. Abuse could also be **emotional,** such as refusing to see the children, making silent telephone calls or trying to scare you; **financial,** such as refusing to pay maintenance, closing a joint bank account or stopping the children's pocket money; or **verbal,** like spreading stories about you or your partner, bad-mouthing you in front of the children or shouting at you.

Families often try to keep domestic abuse hidden but it's important to tell someone what is happening and seek the help and support you need to keep the family safe. Women's Aid is a national organisation that offers a 24-hour helpline and gives advice and support around domestic violence and abuse (see Resources, page 179). This includes advice on your legal rights, how to make a safety plan and how to contact a refuge if you need to get temporary help and shelter. You can also get support from a Relate counsellor or from other organisations in your local area which support those affected by abuse.

WHAT IF YOU DON'T FIND THE RIGHT PERSON?

It's always disappointing when a relationship in which you've invested some time and hope comes to an end, or if you simply don't meet anyone with whom you think you have a future. Did anything go 'wrong' on your dates or were your expectations not met? Look at the experience from an objective perspective, as if you were looking down from above. What could you have done differently, if anything? Is it all working out for the best in the long run?

If you've been keeping up with other friends and interests then you will be disappointed but not devastated. A feeling that you've reached a dead end may be temporary. It gives you a chance to have a break, take stock and enjoy the pleasures of being single; to enjoy your work; to reconnect with family and friends and, if applicable, spend more time with your children. As Dila, 45, said philosophically about her fruitless months of searching: 'Please, no more dating for now! I've got a new obsession with dancing the tango, the waltz and the foxtrot at the moment, and men couldn't be further from my mind.'

When your perspective becomes philosophical, you might want to start getting proactive again, following up fresh profiles and leads to new, interesting people. Or you could take a gentle look inside yourself at the same time and think about your unrealised hopes and dreams. What dreams for the future did you have as a child? What did you want to grow up to be when you were young? Could that point the way forward to a new passion or a new career?

Jim spent some time thinking about this and recalled that, as a child of about 10, he had dreamed of opening a bed and breakfast in a bungalow in the New Forest with his friend, Nin. They would have a big wagon, stacked with hay and pulled by black and golden dogs, which could take the guests down to the nearest shop to get their sweets. Remembering this dream made Jim smile and he didn't mind how crazy it sounded. He signed up to take a residential course in the New Forest where he rekindled a forgotten love of books and watercolour painting, giving him a great sense of accomplishment. Having a balanced life will help you to ride the peaks and troughs of romance.

Chapter 10

Sex

A fulfilling sexual relationship can be the best thing in the world: exciting, tender, passionate, fun, comforting, dangerous, a shelter from the world. The experience of being intimate is something special and unique to us as humans. A good enough sexual relationship forms the 'glue' that keeps many marriages and relationships together. When our work life is hard or we feel careworn, weary or scared about the state of the world, then intimacy and lovemaking help to repair and heal us again.

One of the joys of a new relationship is exploring someone physically and getting to know them through their body: what they like and don't like, what turns them on, how they express their sexuality. As is often said, good sex starts in the head and works south. It's not about technique; it's about a connection of mind and body that is satisfying for both people.

When you're developing a relationship with a new partner, sex may or may not be easy and straightforward. If it is straightforward then that's a bonus, but if you've been out of a relationship for a while, it might be a little more confusing. None of us quite knows what the rules are these days about sex. In a way this is liberating because it offers us a great opportunity to act like assertive adults and try to get in touch with what we really want and what works best for us. If you need to take time before a relationship becomes sexual and you can tell your new partner clearly about this, they will respect your honesty.

From her long experience of interviewing those who are looking for love, Mary Balfour notices great differences between the sexes when it comes to expressing love, sex and closeness. These differences might be partly in our genes and partly the result of the way society conditions the sexes to behave. She sums it up neatly as: 'Men want to be given space, women want to be given intimacy.'

This difference between the sexes causes more friction between women and men than any other part of an intimate relationship. It's almost like there are two love languages in operation, the female and the male. Men tend to want to express intimacy by making love and then get on with doing something else, while women want to express intimacy and closeness *before* they make love and have plenty of cuddling and closeness afterwards too.

Colette and Bill didn't find it easy to be close but they felt drawn to each other. Each had come from families where love wasn't expressed openly and they never saw their parents kissing or hugging. Consequently, they found it hard to 'get going', even though they both felt desire for each other. Eventually, after seeing a counsellor for some sexually focused counselling, they were able to talk more easily about their sexual needs and learned each other's language of love.

Start noticing how you and your partner signal your desire to be close and get intimate. Do you communicate well or are you missing each other's cues? Is there a flow to your intimacy which is enjoyable and fun, or do you get stuck or frustrated when you try and get close or make love? Talk about this and try to understand your partner's way of thinking and how they express their sexuality.

Dominique, a Relate counsellor and colleague, often suggests to couples: 'Never let an opportunity pass by to make love.' She says this because it's easy to let tiredness, annoyance, children, laziness or shyness distract you from being intimate with your partner. And making love can mean whatever you want it to mean; it's not just penetrative sex. It's worth discussing with your partner what you both mean by the phrase 'making love'.

SEX AND THE INTERNET

The Internet isn't just about information and shopping. A recent survey showed that women are most likely to find a potential lover online, with 72 per cent admitting to having had an online romance compared to 52 per cent of men. The report also found that 33 per cent of all online relationships led to a real-world date.

For the less-than-confident individual, the Internet is a wonderful thing because we tend to feel freer to reveal ourselves in front of the computer screen. The shy woman who sits silently through a loud, sociable dinner with friends, feeling she has nothing of interest to say, gets a chance to blossom in a chat room where no-one can see her embarrassment. The socially awkward man who can't bear the idea of going to a noisy party or a nightclub finds himself pleased to be the centre of attention in a chat room about his special hobby.

How many times have less outgoing friends told you they enjoy the anonymity of the Internet and can confide and 'speak' more fluently when they type away on the computer than when they are asked to talk in public? Using e-mail, IM or text is easier than face-to-face or telephone contact in another way: you can take your time to think about your reply instead of getting flustered with an instant answer. Friendships built up slowly over a period of time in chat rooms can often lead to committed real-life relationships. Arguably, the Internet is the greatest ever invention to help shy people come alive and give them a voice. Not to mention those other groups who find it hard to get out of the house because of mobility problems, small children or living in isolated places.

However, Internet communications can make people behave in ways that are out-of-the-ordinary for them. Getting to know someone in cyberspace is different to getting to know someone face-to-face, and it's as well to give this some thought before you get too involved with your online community. A few years back there was a rash of anxiety in the news about affairs and marriage break-ups caused by Internet sites that put you back in touch with old school friends. Not only were old school and college friends chatting in cyberspace, they were also reconnecting via reunion parties and one-to-one meetings. Some of these reunions turned quickly into passionate affairs. At Relate we saw the fallout that these unexpected affairs were having on couples, marriages and children.

One explanation is that in cyberspace we lose all the moral cues that keep us behaving in an adult way in real life, plus all the visual and aural cues we normally use to 'judge' another person: what they look like; their 'status'; their body language, clothes and gestures; their voice. This means that instead of connecting with a real person 'warts and all', we cyber-connect with a childlike part of our own personality, the bit that hasn't become buried under a mountain of adult cares and responsibility.

This cyber-version of ourselves is, in fact, the teenager we would like to have been: a younger-but-wiser, thinner, more attractive, more carefree person than our real selves. As a counsellor, I've lost count of the number of clients who become quite emotional about finding their inner adolescent again. They trick themselves into thinking that their virtual world is just as important as their real-life existence at home with partner, job, mortgage and children. When a husband is upstairs on his computer rescuing fair maidens in a role-playing game while his wife is downstairs cyber-flirting with someone whose avatar looks like Brad Pitt, both of them secretly know that their marriage is in real trouble.

Flirting in cyberspace is the easiest thing in the world because no-one can see the real you: your doubts, your vulnerability or your needs. With a little encouragement, anyone can get carried away with these responsibility-free relationships without realising how much hurt they can do. I think this goes some way to explaining why some love-seekers can get carried away on the Internet: they think they are falling in love with someone on the net but in fact they are falling in love with this carefree, younger and more successful version of themselves. If they do get around to meeting, the budding relationship often can't stand the reality check. A good example is the case of Naomi, a down-to-earth single mother of two teenage girls:

NAOMI (44) *After my marriage ended very messily, I started Internet dating as a way of trying to forget the past and to meet someone decent who would be honest and upright. My profile said I was looking for a 'serious relation-ship', not just 'fun and play'. I thought that men would respect the fact that I'd had a horrible divorce and was feeling a bit bruised and battered by life.*

My first date was pleasant enough but we didn't click at all and neither of us wanted to meet again. Then I got chatting with a lovely-sounding musician who lived in another part of the country, hundreds of miles away, in fact. We shared quite a lot of our feelings and he told me he was feeling bruised too because he had just separated from his wife. We got close very quickly, leading to a few weeks of frantic computer chat and some heavy, erotic flirting over the e-mail – fantastic after a desert of No Sex! It was a tremendous confidence booster and I felt like I'd been reborn as a 20-year-old!

This man invited me to spend a weekend at a country house hotel and, after checking out he was who he said he was and discussing it with my daughters, I agreed to go. It was amazing and we had hours and hours of wonderful Tantric sex, lovely meals, walks around the lake, and plenty of wine. If only it could have carried on because it was such a holiday from my stressful life and I thought we had a really great connection.

I drove home feeling great and phoned him the next morning with a light suggestion about repeating the weekend. His reply: we couldn't meet again because, as he put it, 'We could never recapture those perfect days.' Also, he was going back to his wife.

Though feeling a bit hurt and thinking, 'You're mad – why stop when it's so good!', I still felt quite upbeat and accepted his story. A few weeks later, an Italian friend reappeared on my Facebook page after 20 years, saying: 'My angel, you've come back to me!' Again, we got into some heady Internet flirting, though I was more cautious than the previous time. Again we agreed to meet. After four wonderful days in a Paris hotel, I returned home to find an e-mail saying: 'We cannot do this again. It was TOO good.'

So, through Internet dating, I had two lovely, brief experiences of good sex that boosted my self-esteem at a time when I was the walking-wounded and not ready for a relationship. But am I going to put myself through that again – more Internet dating and more flings? NO WAY!

Although cyberspace relationships can be as lasting and real as any other, don't find yourself being too trusting about what people say and what they do when you meet them via the computer. Remember, they're in love with a fantasy vision of you and a fantasy vision of themselves as lovable.

WHY YOU SHOULD NEVER FALL IN LOVE IN A THUNDERSTORM

When the conditions in which you find yourself falling for someone are arousing and more exciting than real life – like Internet dating – think about the following study. Carried out in 1974, this involved an attractive woman interviewing young men on a suspension bridge over a windy canyon. They were asked to make up a story after seeing a picture of a woman. The study found that they used more sexual imagery than a group of men who were interviewed on a stable wooden bridge. The study concluded that the physical feelings of arousal caused by being on the high suspension bridge intensified the sexual attractiveness of the interviewer.

If you meet someone interesting under arousing conditions – such as an aeroplane take-off, a flirty cyber-chat room or a rock concert – the attraction will be experienced more intensely. The effect is well documented but explanations differ. Many psychologists believe that we associate the arousal of the situation with this person and our own potential for self-improvement and growth. It could also be that the bodily sensations associated with fear, such as shortness of breath and rapid heart rate, are very similar to those associated with love or lust. However, romantic liaisons that have been forged in heightened situations can't always sustain themselves. They tend

> to burn out quickly when faced with the mundane, the routine and the everyday realities of life.

SEX – WHEN IT'S TOO SOON

Naomi's experience of Internet dating (page 163) brings us to the question of how to handle sex if you are trying to develop a lasting relationship. Everyone is different and needs to find their own answers. This question provoked the most passionate debate among the men and women interviewed during the research for this book.

Dylan (36) was able to represent one male point of view – delight in 'the chase':

> *Look, I know this doesn't sound very good but I'm a man and I enjoy the chase. You would be somewhat cheapened in my view if you were willing to sleep with me on the first meeting. When they say 'no' I'm more interested and want to keep seeing them again. During the chase I'm intensely interested in the other person as an individual, what gives her joy. The chase is about building the erotic charge and slowly discovering the other person.*

Dylan, who has had several long-term relationships, spoke for a segment of male opinion in another part of the interview about women's secret agenda:

> *I enjoy Internet dating and am aware that, whatever women say in their profile, they are always interested in lassoing me in. Whatever she says, behind it is Nesting, Mr Right, Forever and 'I'm Only Complete in a Relationship'. I can't be the only man here who doesn't buy all this Settling Down stuff!*

Dylan felt some internal confusion over the question of a lasting relationship because he didn't just want shallow 'fun and play' but to make a deeper, spiritual connection without all the trappings of living together or marriage.

However, 40-year-old Denzil had no time for Dylan's attitude or the way that Internet daters had preyed on Naomi at a time when she was feeling vulnerable and scarred by separation:

> *Men who bonk and run are married. That's the simple answer. It doesn't matter whether or not they take you to a country hotel and wine and dine you first. They want women to like them and they want to be chivalrous but the desire to chase and conquer is testosterone-fuelled and lust is their number-one driver. Why can't they be honest about it?*

Like Dylan, Denzil's previous experiences of marriage had led him to want to avoid that kind of commitment. He wondered how it might be possible to have a relationship without the neediness and vulnerability which he felt came with it:

> *What do I want from a relationship? I want a really clear sense of myself in it. A clear sense of choice to be in it or not. I think you can be addicted to relapsing back into a bad relationship just because it's comfortable and known, but it limits you.*

THE NEVER-ENDING PORRIDGE POT

Jasmine who, with 60 dates behind her, was our most experienced female romance-seeker, memorably described the pull of Internet dating as 'a never-ending porridge pot, a limitless flow of men, women, hope and sex'. She feels she had been hooked, as many seem to get, by the endless possibilities offered by Internet and other modern styles of dating.

> *There is always someone else out there and many are on a carousel of dating. The sort of responses I was getting made me think they were more serious than they turned out to be. The sexual flirting and chat and the sexual encounters were seductive but that scene didn't make me happy. I still want to find a long-term partner.*

Mary Balfour says that, allowing for human desire and the exceptions that prove the rule, if you want a relationship to last, you need to take time to get to know each other before jumping into bed. Allow time to build the erotic tension and a sense of stability. The old saying 'Treat 'em mean to keep 'em keen' still applies, even though it might sound rather manipulative and old-fashioned.

Jasmine has been adventurous in her sexual behaviour and is now seeing a much younger man, but she echoes Mary's words about building a relationship slowly:

> *Good sex that happens quickly doesn't last. Having sex quickly almost separates you from what you want to achieve. My intention was to meet someone and have a kind, loving friendship. The reality was it was kind and loving for two hours or overnight. It was accelerated, fizzing up like a vitamin C tablet, but the bubbles died very quickly. It didn't sustain and feed me like the friendships do.*

Conclusion

W'e've looked at the pleasures – and a few perils – of searching for your ideal mate. All that remains is for me to wish all readers the very best of luck with your search for love. I hope you will flourish in the self-confident glow that comes with feeling good about yourself and being ready to enjoy a happy and fulfilling partnership or marriage.

To sign off, please read Annie's amazing true story of how she met the love of her life in the most unpromising place – a late-night Internet chat room:

I was 43 and had been divorced from my first husband for nine years. A subsequent relationship with someone else was also on its last legs and I was expecting to spend the rest of my life as a single woman. However, one evening, I can't really explain why, I joined a chat room; I think it was a moment of loneliness that made me want some kind of conversation with someone, anyone, male or female. I joined a general chat room. It wasn't specifically a dating site as the LAST thing I wanted in my life was another man!

Whatever I was looking for I didn't find, as many people I 'chatted' with asked for ASL (meaning Age, Sex and Location). Sigh, not the type of conversation I'd hoped for! After an hour or so, I decided the chat room was not for me and put the cursor over the X to sign out forever. Just as I was about to click on the cross, a note came up, just a simple 'Hello'.

I responded by saying that I was just about to turn off the PC as it was late but we could chat for 10 minutes if he wanted. That 10 minutes turned into over an hour.

Over the course of the next three months, that 'chat' progressed to e-mailing regularly, chatting on MSN, using the webcam and making telephone calls. It culminated in us agreeing to meet up in a busy supermarket. I felt I'd found a very good friend and soul mate but, as we lived 200 miles apart, I didn't see how it was possible to form a lasting relationship.

The day we properly met, though, three months after our first click, it was love at first sight. We spent every Sunday, then weekends, then long weekends together until he resigned from work and came to live with me in the Midlands. We were married two years later and are blissfully happy together.

It still amazes me now that we 'found' each other in cyberspace – a split second later and our lives would have taken a very different turn.

Appendix

DATING SAFETY RULES

Follow these rules for dating safely.

1. *Trust your gut intuition.* If you sense something is wrong or the person is dangerous, get out of the situation as soon as possible and, if appropriate, tell the police. Safety is more important than anything.

2. *Make sure that someone knows where you are.* Take a mobile phone with you and let someone know where you are going.

3. *Use a mobile phone to arrange the date.* A landline or office line could be traced to your home or work address.

4. *Never leave a drink unattended or accept a drink from a stranger.* This prevents the potential for a 'date rape' drug being introduced. Remember, too, that heavy drinking will impair your judgement.

5. *Know your sexual limits and state them early on.* If appropriate, let your date know if you are not interested in any sexual involvement.

6. *Be assertive.* Take a self-defence class and feel confident to protect yourself.

7. *Meet in a public place.* Don't be afraid to suggest meeting and separating in a busy place. Don't accept lifts from a stranger or go to their house.

Bibliography

RELATE BOOKS, ESPECIALLY:

Help Your Children Cope with Your Divorce by Paula Hall
  (Vermilion, 2007)
How to Have a Healthy Divorce by Paula Hall
  (Vermilion, 2008)
Loving Yourself, Loving Another by Julia Cole
  (Vermilion, 2001)
Moving On by Suzie Hayman (Vermilion, 2001)
Starting Again by Sarah Litvinoff (Vermilion, 2001)
Step Families by Susan Quilliam (Vermilion, 2001)
The Relate Guide to Better Relationships by Sarah
  Litvinoff (Vermilion, 1992)

BOOKS FOR YOUNG CHILDREN:

Dinosaurs Divorce: A Guide for Changing Families by
  Laurence Krasny Brown and Marc Brown (Little,
  Brown, 1986)

BOOKS FOR PRE-TEENS AND TEENS:

*My Parents are Getting Divorced: How to keep it together
  when your mom and dad are splitting up* by Florence
  Cadier (Harry N Abrams, 2004)
The Suitcase Kid by Jacqueline Wilson (Corgi, 2006)

BOOKS FOR ADULTS:

A Secure Base: Clinical applications of attachment theory by J. Bowlby (Routledge, 1988)

Attachment and Loss, Vol. 1: Attachment by J. Bowlby (Basic Books & Hogarth Press, 1969)

Attachment and Loss, Vol. 2: Separation: Anxiety & anger by J. Bowlby (Basic Books, 1973)

Attachment and Loss, Vol. 3: Loss: Sadness & depression by J. Bowlby (Basic Books, 1980)

Live Alone and Like It by Marjorie Hillia (Virago Press, 2005)

Love Begins at 40 by Cherry Gilchrist and Lara Owen (Hay House, 2008)

Marrying an Older Man by Maggie Jones (Piatkus Books, 1993)

Shared Parenting: Raising your children cooperatively after separation by Jill Burrett and Michael Finch (Finch Publishing, 2007)

Smart Dating – How to Find Your Man by Mary Balfour (Mary Balfour Publications, 2008)

Soulmate Relationships by Ulli Springett (Piatkus Books, 2003)

The Other Side of the Closet: The Coming Out Crisis for Straight Spouses and their Families by Amity Pierce Buxton (John Wiley, 1994)

The Mandates: 25 Real Rules for Successful Gay Dating by Dave Singleton (Random House, 2009)

The Sex Diaries by Bettina Arndt (Melbourne University Press, 2008)

Resources

WEBSITES

www.bbc.co.uk/headroom/wellbeing/guides/rr_socialanxiety.shtml
The BBC's Headroom campaign examines common social anxieties like panic attacks and stress and simple relaxation techniques to reduce them.

www.childline.org.uk
Provides online and telephone support for children of all ages struggling with a wide range of issues.

www.directgov.gov.uk
A public service site providing legal information on divorce and separation.

www.divorceaid.co.uk
A group of professionals providing all-round advice and support on all aspects of separation and divorce, including resources for children and teenagers.

www.insidedivorce.com
Online information site covering all aspects of separation and divorce.

www.inspireparents.com
Jan Powell and Margaret Hickman identify your potential to move through challenging times and put the fun back into family, relationships and finding love.

www.itsnotyourfault.org
Practical information for all family members going
through a break-up.

www.joehoare.co.uk
Joe Hoare runs laughter workshops and talks on the
positive power of laughing.

www.mind.org.uk
The UK's national association for mental health.

www.parentlineplus.org.uk
National charity with decades of experience in supporting
parents and carers via a range of free and flexible services.

www.pinktherapy.com
The UK's largest provider of counselling to lesbian, gay,
bisexual and transgender people.

www.relate.org.uk
Providers of counselling and sex therapy for couples,
families and individuals. You can access relationship
experts face-to-face, by email or by phone. You can also
book onto a course, read about common problems or buy
books online.

www.resolution.org.uk
An organisation of 5,000 family solicitors committed to
resolving separation disputes in a non-confrontational
manner.

www.respect.uk.net
Provides telephone help, information and signposting for
anyone who is worried by domestic violence.

www.saga.co.uk/magazine/relationships
This is a place to look for articles about dating for the
over-50s.

www.wayfoundation.org.uk/index.htm
UK information and forum site for the young and widowed.

www.womensaid.org.uk
Domestic violence charity providing support, advice and temporary accommodation to women, children and men affected by violence or abuse.

www.youngwidow.org
American chat room site for the young and widowed.

ONLINE SELF-HELP

Relate does not recommend or endorse the following websites which do not claim to take the place of one-to-one counselling or medical treatment, but might be a supportive and free place to find peer support.

www.bigwhitewall.com
Calls itself a 'support network for emotional health'. Run by staff and supervised volunteers who try to build a community network of support.

www.horsesmouth.co.uk
Visitors register and search for mentors or befrienders to help with specific life issues. The content of the postings is monitored, and antisocial or unhelpful advice is removed.

Computerised cognitive-behavioural therapy courses are available online at www.beatingtheblues.co.uk for the treatment of mild and moderate depression, and www.fearfighter.com, for panic and phobias. Both are approved by the government and available free through your GP, who has to give you an activation code.

www.livinglifetothefull.com
A Scottish Executive-funded site for depression and

anxiety. It offers a free online course based on CBT which doesn't require a GP referral. The course, authored by Dr Chris Williams, an honorary consultant psychiatrist at Glasgow University, has supported more than 90,000 people and their mental health.

Index